The Advent of Alice

A CELEBRATION OF THE CARROLL CENTENARY

An Exhibition

at the Rosenbach Museum & Library

November 24, 1998 – March 14, 1999

By DIANE WAGGONER

with an essay

by DONALD RACKIN

Edited and with selected entries

by DERICK DREHER

THE ROSENBACH MUSEUM & LIBRARY

PHILADELPHIA

1999

ISBN: 0 939084 31 7

Library of Congress Catalog Card Number 98 - 89292

NATIONAL ENDOWMENT FOR THE
HUMANITIES

Foreword

Seventy years ago, on April 3, 1928, Museum co-founder Dr. A.S.W. Rosenbach purchased at auction the original manuscript to *Alice's Adventures in Wonderland*. "Alice's Adventures under Ground," as it was known, was not the first significant Carroll item the Doctor purchased, nor was it the most expensive book he bought. It was, however, a purchase that stunned Britain and earned him the moniker "The Man Who Bought Alice" in America. Dr. Rosenbach sold the manuscript quickly, but by a quirk of fate, was able to purchase it back in 1946, at which point he and Lessing J. Rosenwald presented it to the British Library as a gift. This story typifies the career of America's preeminent antiquarian dealer: endless swashbuckling acquisitions followed by high-profile sales, balanced by constant generosity toward public collections.

The Rosenbach Museum & Library today preserves one of the world's finest Lewis Carroll collections: over five hundred letters in Charles Dodgson's hand, nearly three dozen original drawings by Sir John Tenniel, rare and often inscribed copies of his books, photographs, and much more. We are extremely fortunate to have been able to win Diane Waggoner, an expert in Victorian art and a student of Carroll in particular, to write the present catalogue. It reflects, if not in every detail, a major exhibition mounted at the Rosenbach. Diane generously agreed to curate the show in a collaborative effort, a task made more difficult both by prestigious research fellowships she obtained almost simultaneously in London and Princeton and the unexpected promotion of the undersigned from curator to director. There should be no mistaking that much of the interpretive work, from the compelling context provided for the objects to their specific evaluations, came from Diane. It is both a duty and a privilege to thank her for her dedication to the project.

Temple professor emeritus Donald Rackin, internationally known for his work on Carroll, kindly agreed to provide an essay on the lasting influence of *Alice* for both children and adults. In so doing—and unbeknownst to the curators at the time the invitation was extended—Don renewed ties with the Rosenbach that date back to the early sixties, when he completed his dissertation research on Dodgson's correspondence with his publisher Macmillan, largely preserved at the Rosenbach. Don has now taken an active role in the Rosenbach's new educational programs, supported in large part by a major grant from the William Penn Foundation. Indeed, this exhibition marks the first flowering of the seeds of outreach sown five years ago by our former director, Stephen K. Urice. Supported by the Rosenbach staff, trustees, members and friends, our director of education Bill Adair has developed a broad range of programs over the past year. The high standard to which we hold our outreach programs ensures that an investment in the Rosenbach is an investment in our community.

A major programming grant from the National Endowment for the Humanities, a federal agency, enabled the exhibition to be developed with a number of additional educational programs. The grant recognizes a unique collaborative effort conceived and administered by the Please Touch Museum (Nancy Kolb, Laura Campbell, Aaron Goldblatt) with the Free Library of Philadelphia (Elliot Shelkrot, Helen Miller, Connie King), our local PBS stations TV12/91FM (Bill Marazzo, Roger Mitchell) and the Rosenbach. The assistance received from these institutions is gratefully acknowledged. Additional support was provided by the Institute of Museum and Library Services, the Pennsylvania Historical and Museum Commission, the Philadelphia Cultural Fund, and The Pew Charitable Trusts. Special gifts were received from The Binswanger Foundation, the Louis N. Cassett Foundation, the Albert M. Greenfield Foundation, The Mary B. & Alvin P. Gutman Fund, Mrs. Lynne Honickman, and Quaker Chemical Foundation.

Christie's, Inc. provided both financial and logistical support for the exhibition, facilitated through the kind offices of Susan D. Ravenscroft and Francis Wahlgren. Additional thanks are due Anna Lou Ashby, Nicolas Barker, John Bidwell, Craig Eisendrath, Eric Fraint, Andrea Immel, Rodney Phillips, Michael Sand, Justin Schiller, and finally Greer Allen, whose design skills are transcended only by his patience.

DERICK DREHER
Director

Introduction

In the late 1940s, a group of American bibliophiles that included Dr. A.S.W. Rosenbach purchased the original manuscript of *Alice's Adventures in Wonderland* from the estate of Eldridge Johnson, sold at the Parke-Bernet Galleries in New York, and presented it to the British Museum "as the slightest token of recognition for the fact that [the British people] held off Hitler while we got ready for war." Accepting the manuscript on behalf of Britain, the Archbishop of Canterbury described the gift as "an unsullied and innocent act in a distracted and sinful world—a pure act of generosity." This little manuscript story of rosy Victorian childhood, written as "A Christmas Gift to a Dear Child in Memory of a Summer Day" by a young Oxford don, had become a myth, representing all that was best about Britain and thus a fitting tribute to the valor of British soldiers. In the twentieth century, "Alice" is indeed greater than the sum of her parts, a fictional heroine that has become one of the world's most instantly recognizable child-figures, appearing in countless films, theatrical productions, postcards, books, and games, and as a toy and other assorted products. As one of the most widely translated and quoted books in the English language, *Alice's Adventures in Wonderland* has long been one of Britain's biggest cultural exports.

Since *Alice's* inception in 1862, the United States has always been one of the most hospitable consumers of this export. Lewis Carroll sent the rejected printings of his books here on several occasions, Disney produced the most famous film version of *Alice*, and American collectors, including Dr. Rosenbach, amassed the largest collections of Lewis Carroll material in the world. For a time, of course, the manuscript itself had been a famous American import: Dr. Rosenbach had already purchased the original manuscript once before in 1928 at auction from its first owner, Alice Pleasance Hargreaves, née Liddell, the "real" Alice.

Despite its trans-Atlantic and trans-historical appeal today, the story of *Alice* is rooted in the specific circumstances of upper middle-class Victorian England. Alice's adventures are also those of her creator, Lewis Carroll, whom we now commemorate on the hundredth anniversary of his death. Behind *Alice* is the now famous story of Lewis Carroll's friendship with Alice Liddell, a friendship invoked in his poignant prefatory and closing poems to the two *Alice* books. And behind the pseudonym Lewis Carroll is Charles L. Dodgson, a bachelor Oxford don and Anglican deacon, friend of children, vigorously involved with the literature, art, and theater of his day as well as his chosen profession of mathematics and avocation as an amateur photographer. Copious documentation of his life survives in his diaries and a vast number of letters and manuscripts. Sir John Tenniel, the illustrator of *Alice's Adventures in Wonderland* and *Alice's* other creator, should be mentioned too, as he fashioned the familiar golden-haired little girl in her bell-shaped dress and pinafore.

What should we make of Lewis Carroll today? In his introductory essay, Donald Rackin shows that Carroll's life and work can teach us to treat children with respect. Yet Carroll's star of notoriety has also been rising. In an age of heightened awareness of suspect images of children and pedophilia, we can easily imagine Carroll as a ready-made Victorian precedent for such concerns. We scrutinize his parade of little girls before the camera lens, his identification of the prepubescent female nude as the ideal of beauty, or the myriad letters he wrote to his ever-growing flock of child-friends with very different eyes than his contemporaries, including his own child-friends. Debate on the proper reading of such evidence has been carried out in several recent biographies and newspaper articles, and I leave to them the attempt to determine Carroll's inner life. In this exhibition, I wish to let the objects and texts speak for themselves. I have tried to explain the context of the objects within Carroll's life and the culture of his time in order to give the reader a base from which to draw his or her own conclusions. All letters are understood to be signed autographs unless otherwise noted.

The material Dr. Rosenbach acquired has largely determined the themes of this exhibition. His interest focused specifically on the genesis of *Alice* and Carroll's corpus of publications and letters. He did not seek to acquire *Alice's* many translations, parodies, or later editions illustrated by artists other than Tenniel. He eschewed Carroll's photographs. Later acquisitions—the Hatch and Miller collections from former child-friends, and the Carroll–Frost correspondence and Frost drawings—have added to the rich material acquired by Dr. Rosenbach and broadened the collections in significant ways.

The exhibition is divided into eight sections. These sections do not present a comprehensive portrait of Carroll's life: certain aspects, such as his mathematics, his activities within the Oxford community, and his religious beliefs, have largely been omitted. Other aspects such as his interest in the theater and visual arts are touched upon only in passing. Carroll's photogra-

ROBINSON & CHERRILL.   TUNBRIDGE WELLS.

2. Charles L. Dodgson, self-portrait photograph, inscribed to A.B. Frost,
ca. March 1874

phy, too, only appears sporadically: the Rosenbach hopes to mount a second exhibition devoted to this topic in the coming years. After a brief introductory section about Carroll, incorporating portraits and personal artifacts, the next several sections focus on *Alice's Adventures in Wonderland*: first, the friendship between Carroll and Alice Liddell, the inspiration for Carroll's story; second, Tenniel's illustrations which established *Alice* in our collective visual imagination; third, the history of the publication of the books and Carroll's relationship with his publisher; and fourth, Alice Liddell's life after *Alice*. Alice, later Mrs. Reginald Hargreaves, had only occasional adult contact with Carroll. But ironically, it was only as an adult that she became famous as Carroll's inspiration. On the centenary of Carroll's birth in 1932, she journeyed to America and was catapulted out of obscurity into the American press. The second half of the exhibition turns to Carroll's life after *Alice* with letters to his later child-friends, the games and puzzles he produced for them, his subsequent books for children, and finally, the tale of Carroll's relationship with another one of his illustrators, the American A.B. Frost. Most of these letters from Carroll to Frost have never been published before.

In putting together the exhibition, many people have made invaluable contributions. I wish first to thank Derick Dreher, first curator and then director of the Rosenbach, for giving me the opportunity to work with the collection and for sharing both his office and his expertise. Other staff members at the Rosenbach—in particular Bill Adair, Jason Staloff, Elizabeth Fuller, Catherine Hitchens, and Holly Victor—always readily offered their help and support. Gratitude is also due to an anonymous private collector; David Schaefer; and the New York Public Library, all of whom have kindly lent items from their collections.

Anyone working on Lewis Carroll today owes a great debt to the eminent scholars who have unearthed a wealth of information on Carroll, the people he knew, and his books. I wish to single out in particular Edward Wakeling, Selwyn Goodacre, Anne Clark, and of course, Morton N. Cohen, for their contributions to Carroll studies. A special thank you goes to Edward Wakeling as well for personally sharing his knowledge of Carroll's photography. And thank you to my fellow scholars, friends, and family who offered their help. Donald Rackin, Jennifer L. Roberts, Emma Prunty, Susan L. Smits, Lawrence Waggoner, and Lynne Waggoner all gave their time to provide insightful comments on the text.

DIANE WAGGONER

"What is the use of a book … ?"
Useful and Instructive Lessons from Lewis Carroll

By Donald Rackin

Lewis Carroll's reputation as a pioneer in children's literature has grown steadily ever since the publication in 1865 of *Alice's Adventures in Wonderland*—particularly because of his rejection of the long tradition that treated books for children primarily as instruments of instruction rather than as sources of simple delight. In his earliest literary efforts and throughout much of his career, Carroll's best comic effects often depend on playful spoofs, both blatant and subtle, of the didactic, moralistic strain that dominated children's reading materials throughout the nineteenth century.

Twenty years before *Wonderland*, the thirteen-year-old Charles Dodgson had produced for the entertainment of his younger siblings a charming little manuscript volume of sixteen comic poems, *Useful and Instructive Poetry* (circa 1845). Embellished by hand-colored illustrations and such conclusions as "Moral: 'Don't dream'" and "Moral: 'Don't stew your sister,'" this book already manifested the unmistakable Carrollian genius for satirical—and sometimes violent—parodies of such doggedly useful and instructive texts. That genius reached its zenith in his mature *Alice* books, in which fantastic adventures and pure fun—certainly not moral lessons for children—seem the sole purpose of the tales; where, for instance, the silly Ugly Duchess is made even sillier because, as Alice puts it, she is so "fond . . . of finding morals in things!" and where such a venerable fixture of juvenile moral instruction as Isaac Watts' poem "Against Idleness and Mischief" (from his *Divine Songs for Children*, 1715) is deftly subverted by transforming Watts' familiar paragon of harmless natural industry, the busy little bee who "improve[s] each shining hour," into Alice's grinning, Darwinian crocodile who "improve[s] his shining tail" as he graciously opens his "gently smiling jaws" to "welcome . . . little fishes in."

Such telling subversions of moralistic and utilitarian children's literature occur with particular frequency in Alice's underground adventures (where her aboveground, rote-learned lessons are pointedly useless, failing her just when she turns to them to re-establish her fragile identity). Indeed, this curious child's very first words—"and what is the *use* of a book . . . without pictures and conversations?" (my italics)—function emblematically, encapsulating at the outset an implicit argument of this ostensibly uninstructive, "useless" dream-book with its fantastic pictures and hilariously pointless conversations. Moreover, besides making parodic fun out of Alice's misremembrances of insipid schoolroom poetry, *Wonderland* also satirizes the widespread Victorian custom of subjecting young readers of fiction to "nice little stories," as the adult narrator wryly calls them, "about children who had got burnt, and eaten up by wild beasts and other unpleasant things, all because they *would* not remember the simple rules their friends had taught them."

Thirty years after *Useful and Instructive Poetry*, Carroll was still addressing these issues with characteristic irony. Although his nihilistic *Hunting of the Snark* (1876) is hardly as well suited for child readers as it is for adults, it nevertheless fits the same general pattern, immediately presenting itself as a zany and pointless send-up of a morally instructive quest tale, especially in its satiric parallels with Coleridge's long, heavily didactic *Rime of the Ancient Mariner* (1798). Carroll begins his preface to the *Snark* by facetiously referring to himself as "the author of this brief but instructive poem." He then declares, "I will not (as I might) point to the strong moral purpose of this poem," a moral purpose of which, some ten years later, he publicly declared complete ignorance:

> Periodically, I have received courteous letters from strangers, begging to know whether "The Hunting of the Snark" is an allegory, or contains some hidden moral, or is a political satire: and for all such questions, I have but one answer, "*I don't know!*"
> —"Alice on the Stage," 1887

Further complicating the issue are coy remarks like these in an 1884 letter to the Lowrie children:

> As to the meaning of the Snark? I'm very much afraid I didn't mean anything but nonsense! Still, you know, words mean more than we mean to express when we use them: so a whole book ought to mean a great deal more than the writer meant. So, whatever good meanings are in the book, I'm very glad to accept as the meaning of the book.

In the same letter Carroll also writes:

> . . . a "Lady Superior" . . . wrote to ask to see a copy of *Alice* before accepting it: for she had to be

12. John Tenniel, "The Pool of Tears," pencil drawing, 1865

very careful, all the children [in her hospital] being Roman Catholics, as to what "religious reading" they got! I wrote to say, "You shall certainly see it first, if you like: but I can guarantee that the [*Alice*] books have no religious teaching in them—in fact, they do not teach anything at all."

NEVERTHELESS, despite such puzzling contradictions, sly disavowals and droll evasions, despite all the apparently meaningless "nonsense" in Carroll's literary creations, his three greatest fantasies—the two *Alice*s and the *Snark*—are themselves fundamentally useful and instructive. Although some literary scholars persist in claiming that Carroll's surreal masterpieces derive their power from their liberating free play and their refreshing absence of all applicable meaning or moral significance, such a view fails to square with several irrefutable facts. First, there is the by now almost universal acceptance of the general principles of the unconscious and dream signification: Freudians and anti-Freudians alike now subscribe to the ancient conception of dreams and fantasies as rich sources of meaning and invaluable clues to the hidden workings of the dreamer's psyche; hence, Alice's seemingly random, pointless and laughable dreams are now often read as covert, dramatized revelations of her (or her creator's, or sometimes even her readers') innermost anxieties and desires. Next, there is the large and growing body of interpretive work that since the 1930s has, in scores of insightful scholarly and critical studies, demonstrated how meaningful and morally significant these ostensibly silly fantasies actually are. Finally—and most important—there is the fact that today, one hundred years after their author's death, the *Alice*s (translated into over seventy languages) are more revered than ever around the world as mythic repositories of oddly practical wisdom and instructive wit. Indeed, hardly a day passes when one does not encounter allusions to Alice's dreams in the most sober and serious observations of eminent thinkers in virtually every discipline and cultural setting. Thus, for example, the Red Queen's ridiculous declaration that in her country "it takes all the running *you* can do, to keep in the same place" has become something of a universal motto for our frenetic lives; while for many readers, Alice's insistent cry "'Who in the world am I?' Ah *that's* the great puzzle!" frames with Carrollian conciseness the principal existential problem of our age.

This is not to say, of course, that Carroll's masterpieces always speak in exactly the same ways to both children and adults. Martin Gardner's indispensable edition, *The Annotated Alice* (1960), has demonstrated that the books are generously laced with covert references to all sorts of matters (historical, mathematical, scientific, linguistic, and philosophical) beyond the ken of even the most sophisticated child reader. But that in no way vitiates the argument that they provide important instruction for children as well as for adults, instruction conveyed through vivid experiences and dramatic examples rather than by rote-learned rules and pedestrian moral precepts. As Alice herself points out when the Red Queen suggests that Alice has "not had many lessons in manners," "Manners are not taught in lessons. . . . Lessons teach you to do sums, and things of that sort."

In his recent authoritative biography, Morton Cohen succinctly describes the central meaning of Alice's underground journey: "*Wonderland*," Cohen writes, "illustrates how a young, inexperienced person can deal with this inexplicably chaotic world and survive as part of it." For the practical truth *Wonderland* illustrates for all its readers, young or old, is essential: if one perseveres, even when confronted by authentic dream-visions of the mad and frightful chaos beneath the conscious grounds of constructed order, one can—like the heroic child Alice—dispel those visions, return to that constructed above-ground world, and thereby survive whole and sane. Similarly, *Looking-Glass* (with its much more mature heroine) shows readers how to play the game "being played," as Alice says, "all over the world"; how, like Alice, to manage with compassion, grace and good manners in life's unavoidable encounters with exasperating, childish adults seemingly bent on impeding their progress towards maturity and integration ("manage" is a frequently recurring, pivotal term in Alice's looking-glass adventures).

In other words, Alice plays the role of the reader's surrogate. Her quests for the Edenic, "loveliest garden" and for the autonomy of queenhood serve as vicarious dream adventures for readers of all ages who, usually without realizing it, employ these mythic adventures—brilliantly presented as mere random, absurd entertainments—as precious and durable survival manuals. For, by means of her reactions to her maddening dream adventures beneath the ground and behind the mirror, Carroll's plucky heroine unwittingly provides his readers with a number of eminently useful object-lessons in the arts of psychic and social survival. Viewed in this light, "useful" and "instructive" ironically become precisely the right terms to describe these books so often admired for their uncannily accurate representations of the dream state and the therapeutic dynamics of dream-work. And the sudden conclusions of these dreams are equally instructive: at the limits of her patience and inner resources, Alice awakes, instinctively ending her vivid dreams by dispelling, for the moment, the "dreadful confusion" and the threatening demons of her own powerful, unconscious imagination, relegating them by means of (albeit now shaky) above-ground language to unthreatening categories like mere chessmen or "nothing but a pack of cards!" and labeling her luminous adventures with insipid terms like "curious," "wonderful" and "such a nice dream."

The notion that, despite their overt rejections of didacticism, Carroll's great fantasies teach unfantastic truths should come as no surprise to readers familiar with his complex personality and his fascination with reversals of all sorts—in mirrors and mirror-writing, puns and portmanteau words, lens images and the negative/positive processes of photography, and the inherent contradictions of his own dual identities. After all, Lewis Carroll (the ineffectual Dodo and White Rabbit of *Wonderland*, the old and ridiculously inept White Knight of *Looking-Glass*) was at the same time a conservative and respectable clergyman/don—the Reverend Charles Lutwidge Dodgson, M.A., Senior Student and Mathematical Lecturer of Christ Church, Oxford—by profession, both a teacher and a preacher. But, unlike the conventional teachers and preachers of his time, he was also acutely conscious of the pedagogical value of combining instruction with amusement, work with play, laughter with serious reflection. In fact, he invented a number of instructive games for both children and adults; and the *Alice*s themselves are loosely based on games Carroll taught his young charges and played with them—cards and croquet first, chess when they were older.

Eight or Nine Wise Words about Letter-Writing (1890) provides a good example of how—even in unambiguously instructive works like *Symbolic Logic* (1896), which he called a "healthy mental recreation," or *The Game of Logic* (1886), which he used as a textbook while teaching classes of girls—Carroll characteristically combined teaching with entertainment. Accompanied by the fanciful *Wonderland Postage-stamp Case* and ostensibly directed at children, this amusing pamphlet offers, even today, very practical instruction for conscientious letter-writers regardless of their ages: detailed, thoughtful advice from one of the world's most prolific and brilliant correspondents, whose many delightful letters to young girls include some of the finest examples of his inimitable humor, as well as his passionate devotion to the edification of countless child-friends.

Carroll's ninth rule in *Wise Words* illustrates his rare talent for producing playful fusions of conversational intimacy, delicious absurdity, simple laughter, and practical instruction. Warning against the practice of cross-writing (i.e. writing cross-wise over one's own writing in order to save paper and/or postage costs), Carroll writes:

> When you get to the end of a note-sheet, and find you have more to say, take another piece of paper —a whole sheet, or a scrap, as the case may demand: but whatever you do, *Don't cross!* Remember the old proverb *"Cross-writing makes cross reading."* "The *old* proverb?" you say, inquiringly. "*How* old?" Well, not so *very* ancient, I must confess. In fact, I'm afraid I invented it while writing this paragraph! Still, you know, "old" is a *comparative* term. I think you would be *quite* justified in addressing a chicken, just out of the shell, as "Old boy!", *when compared* with another chicken, that was only half-out!

Among the principal virtues of the *Alice*s, then, is that they are at once both adult and children's books. And it is here that Carroll's reputation as a pioneer in children's literature seems fully justified and secure. For, besides subverting the conventional dividing lines between adulthood and childhood, his imaginative writings play a major role in the modern breakdown of strict and confining literary genres—arbitrary categories that artificially separate high art from popular art, magic and fantasy from realism, the absurd from the serious, and adult books from children's books.

To a great extent, the success of the *Alice* books comes from their ability to speak simultaneously to both child and adult audiences, as, for instance, when an adult reads them aloud to a child. Carroll realized that, in order to achieve their full potential, his books for children must stimulate, entertain, and even edify the adult reader as well. Hence, he provides both *Alice*s with a distinct, obviously grown-up, humorous and somewhat ironic narrator, as well as a number of covert allusions to matters only adults would comprehend. It should be remembered in this context that the entire *Alice* project began simply as an extemporary tale told leisurely by Dodgson to the Liddell sisters *and* to Robinson Duckworth, an Oxford friend and the other grown-up on that famous July 4 expedition in 1862—all in the same boat. The Rosenbach copy of the 1886 facsimile edition of *Alice's Adventures under Ground* (Carroll's first written version of *Wonderland*) is inscribed to Duckworth: "the Duck from the Dodo," thus attesting to the fact that, from the beginning, the *Alice*s were made to engage their two distinct audiences.

In fact, Carroll's life itself can still teach something basic for adults, a golden rule that the exasperatingly childish, grown-up inhabitants of Alice's dreams have obviously not learned: children deserve the same respect that adults do. The full effectiveness of Carroll's satires of didactic children's literature (and the Victorian middle-class treatment of children generally) frequently depends on the sense of equality and shared intimacy he immediately establishes with his young readers. He is, they infer, dependably on their side. Edith Rowell, one of Carroll's erstwhile child-friends, said many years after his death that when she was a child, "He gave me a sense of my own dignity." That effect still shines through innumerable letters Carroll wrote to children, wherein one is hard-pressed to detect traces of adult condescension, of Carroll talking down to his young—sometimes very young—correspondents. Even Carroll's uncompromising standards for the production of his children's books demonstrate this enormous esteem for children: the early *Alice* editions are, among other things, models of the most meticulous, painstaking attention and care (with costly production changes that were sometimes paid for out of Carroll's own pocket). Carroll's frequent use of the term "child-friend" also bespeaks this respect for children's personal dignity: six months before he died, he wrote, "I'd rather have *one* child-*friend* than a thousand child-*admirers*."

This manifest respect for children emanates, it could be said, from a kind of healthy self-respect. For Carroll never lost sight of the precious (and sometimes frightened) child who remained alive within him—as it does in most adults—the wondering child who still dreamed his dreams and continued to ask, as Einstein has put it, "childish" questions about such things as Time and Space. In Carroll's own case, this child within was sometimes the stuttering little Charles Dodgson who was warned, in *Useful and Instructive Poetry*, "Learn well your grammar, | And never stammer," and sometimes the playful and laughing child whose "happy summer days" he always longed to recapture.

Thus, the *Alice* books provide for their adult readers a very special instructive experience. As Virginia Woolf has said, "childhood lodged in [Carroll] whole and entire," so "he could do what no one else has ever been able to do—he could return to that [childhood] world; he could create it, so that we too become children again." Accordingly, the *Alices* draw adult audiences fully into the reading and dreaming experiences, providing the way for grown-ups to share once more in childhood's wonder. In other words, Carroll's best works enable adult readers, through a rejuvenation of their withered imaginations, to attain for the moment the goal for which the twenty-one-year-old Carroll already hungered:

> I'd give all wealth that years have piled,
> The slow result of Life's decay
> To be once more a little child
> For one bright summer-day.
> —"Solitude," 1853

Carroll's prefatory poem to *Through the Looking-Glass*, addressed to an Alice estranged from him and now approaching twenty, could very well be read as a piece of useful and instructive poetry. Speaking directly to Alice, the nearly forty-year-old Carroll says, with a tinge of bitter irony and foreboding, "We are but older children, dear | Who fret to find our bedtime near." Such an ominous statement may not seem an appropriate opening for a child's book. But considering what the book that follows is about and the dual audience it addresses, these two lines seem just right, reflecting as they do for the adult Alice, Carroll's most intimate thoughts and feelings about the child within each of us and the close links between children and adults—forged, to a great extent, by their shared mortality.

It is particularly fitting that the many important commemorations of this year's Carroll centenary conclude at the Rosenbach Museum & Library, home of one of the world's finest Carroll collections. For, besides the fact that Dr. Rosenbach was a great scholar and collector of children's books, his home was for several short periods up until 1947 the repository of the most precious of all Carrollian artifacts—*Alice's Adventures under Ground* (1864), the beautiful manuscript volume (now in the British Library) that Charles Dodgson himself painstakingly hand-lettered and illustrated as his first "love-gift of a fairy-tale" for his beloved child-friend, Alice Liddell. It is also fitting that the current Rosenbach exhibition focuses on Alice: the real girl and woman, the cultural institution, the archetypal child-heroine, and the adoring fantasy creation of a fertile and unique imagination. This focus underscores what we celebrate on such an occasion: One hundred years after his death and nearly one hundred and forty years after her first appearance as the heroine of the world's most famous book addressed to both children and adults, Lewis Carroll and his beloved Alice grow, year after year, more instructive, more alive than ever.

The Reverend Charles Lutwidge Dodgson,
Alias "Lewis Carroll"

BORN IN 1832 in Daresbury, Cheshire, Charles Lutwidge Dodgson was the eldest son in the large family of the curate Charles Dodgson (1800–68). After a typical middle-class upbringing in which he was sent away to school, Dodgson matriculated at Christ Church, Oxford, in 1850. He took up residence at Christ Church in 1851 and it remained his home for the rest of his life, a total of forty-seven years. Dodgson obtained a Studentship (the equivalent of a Fellowship at other colleges) in 1852. Once appointed, a Student could hold the position for life as long as he met the double requirements to stay unmarried and to be ordained a priest in the Church of England. While Dodgson never married, he did not in fact wish to take holy orders, and he convinced the Dean of Christ Church to allow him to keep his studentship even though he proceeded only so far as ordination in 1861 as a deacon rather than as a priest.

DODGSON distinguished himself in mathematics while he was an undergraduate. In 1855, he was appointed Mathematical Lecturer, a post he retained until he resigned in 1881. Dodgson was a man of many more interests, though. He became an excellent amateur photographer, read avidly on many subjects, took a lively interest in art, and maintained a lifelong passion for the theater. Although he lived his entire adult life in the cloistered confines of Christ Church, he made frequent trips to London and the seaside and cultivated (and photographed) a wide circle of friends that included prominent academics, writers, artists, and actors. Alongside these numerous adult friends, Dodgson established a continuous string of friendships with children, usually little girls. Children were central to his emotional life. Like many of his contemporaries, Dodgson saw children as offering solace to the adult mind through their beauty, innocence, and purity, but he also prized the individuality and behavioral freedom of children. While a young man, Dodgson befriended Alice Liddell, the daughter of the Dean of Christ Church and his "ideal child-friend," as he would later describe her. She inspired *Alice's Adventures in Wonderland*, the book that brought Dodgson fame as a master of nonsense under the pseudonym Lewis Carroll. He went on to write a sequel, *Through the Looking-glass: and what Alice found there*, other books for children, mathematical works, and poetry. Dodgson died of bronchitis at the age of 65 on January 14, 1898.

1 PHOTOGRAPH
Charles L. Dodgson, Self-portrait

Not dated, but circa May 1875
Albumen print mounted on a carte-de-visite
Inscribed on verso: "Emily Kerr | from Lewis Carroll" in purple ink

DODGSON PROBABLY arranged this composition himself and had someone else remove and replace the lens cap to take the photograph. Emily Kerr, a cousin of the Hatch family who were Oxford friends of Dodgson's, sent Dodgson a photograph of herself and her sister in 1871. Dodgson is known to have corresponded with Kerr in 1871 and 1873.

ALTHOUGH this particular image bears neither a date nor other identifying marks, Dodgson numbered many of his photographs and such a number can be found on another print of this photograph. That number suggests the year 1875, when Dodgson would have been forty-three.

INVENTED in the 1830s, photography had become cheap, quick and easily accessible to the public by the 1870s. Once the province of only the most prosperous, portraiture was now widely available through the proliferation of photographic studios. As with this carte-de-visite given to Emily Kerr, exchanging and collecting photographs of famous people, friends, and acquaintances became an integral part of Victorian society. Over the course of his lifetime, Dodgson avidly made and collected portraits. He took several photographs of himself and had his photograph taken both by fellow amateurs and professional photographers.

2 PHOTOGRAPH
Charles L. Dodgson, Self-portrait

Not dated, but circa March 1874
Albumen print mounted on a carte labeled Robinson & Cherrill, Tunbridge Wells
Inscribed on verso: "A.B. Frost, Esq. | from the Artist & Victim, | Lewis Carroll. | May 2/78"

DODGSON presents himself as a man of letters in this self-portrait photograph probably printed and mounted for Dodgson from his own negative by Robinson & Cherrill, a commercial photograph studio. It was taken when he was forty-two, according to the

1. Charles L. Dodgson, self-portrait
inscribed to Emily Kerr, ca. May 1875

serial number on another print of this photograph. Dodgson sent the image to A.B. Frost, the American artist illustrating his book of comic poems *Rhyme? and Reason?*. The following day Dodgson wrote to Frost,

> One thing I forgot to ask you when I gave you my photograph, which was never to let it out of your own possession. If a photographer got hold of it, and copied it, it would be a great annoyance to me: I specially wish my *face* to remain unknown to the public. I like my *books* to be known, of course: but *personally* I hope to remain in obscurity. Please don't show it (except to your own friends): I mean, don't put it where casual strangers can see it.[1]

EVEN THOUGH Dodgson pursued the acquaintance of distinguished men and women and sought or took their photographs, he professed a horror of being 'lionized' himself, a Victorian term for celebrity-worship. Despite pride in his fame as Lewis Carroll, captured in this photograph and his inscription to Frost, Dodgson went to great lengths to conceal his true identity to the public at large. He often denied to strangers that he had any connection with Lewis Carroll. Nevertheless, Dodgson's friends knew of his alter ego, which he sometimes used as a means of making further acquaintances.

1. Letter from Charles L. Dodgson to A.B. Frost, 3 May 1878, Rosenbach Museum & Library.

3 MANUSCRIPT

Charles L. Dodgson, so-called 'Picture Book'

Not dated, but circa 1844
Pen and ink and watercolor on paper
See illustration inside back wrapper

ONE OF THE VERY earliest surviving documents of the life (and sense of humor) of Dodgson, this undated collection of visual puns and silly pictures was probably created by Dodgson for his sisters. Dates as early as 1841—when the author would have been nine years old—and as late as 1850 have been suggested for the Picture Book; a date between the two seems most likely. The drawing reproduced here depicts two policemen chasing a top-hatted thief. Below, three figures in antiquated court dress offer up commentaries on the doublet, "And all was for a pudding he took, | And from the cook of Colnbrook." These figures are impressively rendered, particularly with respect to their foreshortening, and it has been suggested that Dodgson's older sisters assisted him in the effort.

4 PASSPORT

Foreign Office, Great Britain, Passport for Charles L. Dodgson

1867
Dark brown leather with flap closure and gilt-stamped lettering "Revd. Charles L. Dodgson."

DODGSON TRAVELED extensively through England, spending lengthy vacations at the seaside in particular. He obtained this passport for the only journey he made outside his native country, a two-month trip with his close friend Henry Parry Liddon, a fellow Student at Christ Church and subsequently Canon and Chancellor of St. Paul's Cathedral in London. The two traveled through Brussels, Cologne, and Berlin to St. Petersburg and Moscow, where they spent the bulk of their time. On the return journey they passed through Warsaw, Breslau, Dresden, Ems, and Bingen. They stayed a week in Paris, where they saw the Universal Exhibition. At their various destinations, Dodgson and Liddon visited cathedrals and churches and debated the merits of the elaborate rituals of Catholicism and Eastern Orthodoxy. They also marveled at architecture, went to art galleries, and occasionally witnessed local customs and ceremonies, such as a visit to a Jewish synagogue in Berlin and a Russian wedding.[1] Dodgson's passport bears both German and Russian stamps, but does not contain a physical description of the passport holder.

2. For excerpts from Dodgson's diary of the journey, see John Francis McDermott, ed., *The Russian Journal and other Selections from the works of Lewis Carroll* (New York, 1935), and from Liddon's, see Morton N. Cohen, *The Russian Journal—II: A Record Kept by Henry Parry Liddon of a Tour Taken with C.L. Dodgson in the Summer of 1867* (New York, 1979).

5 WATCH

A. Bach of London, Pocket watch

Hallmarked 1868
Silver case with inlaid enamel numerals. Engraved: "Rev. C.L. Dodgson | CH. CH. OXFORD." Private collection

THIS IS ONE of two pocket watches owned by Dodgson that has survived, and the only one in a private collection. Time fascinated the mathematician and logician in Dodgson. He writes of time in many of his letters and formulated numerous puzzles. The subject also recurs frequently in his books. *Alice's Adventures in Wonderland*, for example, features the White Rabbit consulting his watch and the Mad Hatter musing on butter having ruined a watch's works.

Alice's Origins
The Dodo, the Duck, and the Dean's Daughters

"It was high time to go, for the pool was getting quite crowded with the birds and animals that had fallen into it: there was a Duck and a Dodo, a Lory and an Eaglet"

—Lewis Carroll, *Alice's Adventures in Wonderland*

THE STORY of *Alice* originated in Dodgson's friendship with the three eldest daughters of Henry George Liddell (1811–98), co-author of the Liddell–Scott Greek–English lexicon. Dodgson was a young man of twenty-four when Liddell was appointed Dean of Christ Church and moved his family there in 1855. At the time, his family consisted of his wife, née Lorina Reeve (1826–1910), Harry (1847–1911), Lorina (1849–1930), Alice (1852–1934), and Edith (1854–76). Alice, aged three, first met "Mr. Dodgson" when he photographed Christ Church Cathedral from the garden of the Deanery in April 1856.

THE FRIENDSHIP with the Liddell sisters soon became very important to Dodgson. Although not the only children with whom he spent time even at this early stage in his life, Lorina, Alice and Edith were clearly the child-friends he cherished most. On the untimely death of Edith in 1876, Dodgson looked back to describe the Liddells as "the most intimate child-friends I ever had."[1] The volumes of his diary covering the period April 1858 to May 1862, when their friendship initially developed, do not survive. But from 1862 until 1863, when the friendship suffered a rupture, Dodgson's diaries are filled with entries about visits with the three girls. There are walks around Oxford, games of croquet in the Deanery garden, photograph sessions, birthday gifts, and boating excursions on the river accompanied by one or another male friend of Dodgson's and sometimes the Liddells' governess. As the prefatory poem to *Alice's Adventures in Wonderland* describes, the story was first told "all in the golden afternoon" during one of those boat trips, up the river to Godstow. Robinson Duckworth, a Fellow at Trinity College and friend of Dodgson's, was the fifth member of the party that day.

1. Letter to Mrs. J. Chataway in Morton N. Cohen, ed., with Roger Lancelyn Green, *The Letters of Lewis Carroll*, 2 vols. (Oxford, 1979), p. 254.

6 PHOTOGRAPH

Charles L. Dodgson, "Open your mouth, and bob for a cherry" (Edith, Lorina, and Alice Liddell)

1860. Albumen print

DODGSON'S primary hobby from 1856 to 1880 was photography. Despite the complicated procedure during the early decades of the technology, Dodgson became adept at this new means of producing images. One of many photographs Dodgson took of the Liddell sisters, this image was produced in July 1860, two years before the famous river trip of 1862. Mrs. Liddell often dressed her daughters in identical outfits and here Dodgson arranged them in a tableau of arrested action, playing a simple children's game. Six-year-old Edith sits on the table holding the cherries in her lap. Eleven-year-old Lorina dangles cherries in front of the mouth of eight-year-old Alice, who stands with her eyes closed. Dodgson printed smaller versions of this photograph cropped more closely around the figures of the three girls, sometimes labeled "Open your mouth and shut your eyes." Photography and

6. Charles L. Dodgson, "Open your mouth, and bob for a cherry," photograph, 1860

storytelling went hand in hand for Dodgson, both in the narrative aspect of this particular photograph and in the process of taking it. Alice Liddell claimed years later that many of the episodes Dodgson used for *Through the Looking-Glass* stemmed from the stories he told to amuse the little girls in order to put them in the right mood to pose for the camera.[1]

1. Alice P. Hargreaves and Caryl Hargreaves, "Alice's Recollections of Carrollian Days, as Told to her Son," *Cornhill Magazine,* July 1932, pp. 1–12. Partially reprinted in *Alice in Wonderland. Norton Critical Edition,* ed. Donald J. Gray (New York, 1992) and Morton N. Cohen, ed., *Lewis Carroll: Interviews and Recollections* (London, 1989).

7 BOOK

Catherine Sinclair, *Holiday House*

London: Simpkin, Marshall, & Co., [2nd ed. 1856]
Inscribed on fly-leaf: "L.A. and E. Liddell | a Christmas gift | from C.L. Dodgson" with acrostic poem spelling "Lorina, Alice, Edith"
Courtesy of New York Public Library, Berg Collection

> Little maidens, when you look
> On this little story-book,
> Reading with attentive eye
> Its enticing history,
> Never think that hours of play
> Are your only HOLIDAY,
> And that in a HOUSE of joy
> Lessons serve but to annoy:
> If in any HOUSE you find
> Children of a gentle mind,
> Each the others pleasing ever—
> Each the others vexing never—
> Daily work and pastime daily
> In their order taking gaily—
> Then be very sure that they
> Have a *life* of HOLIDAY.
>
> Christmas 1861

DODGSON PRESENTED this book to the Liddell sisters in 1861. The inscription is a rare surviving document of the friendship between Dodgson and the Liddell girls, as Mrs. Liddell later destroyed his early letters to the children. By writing an acrostic of his friends' first names, Dodgson asks the children to discover their own names 'hidden' in the poem in addition to reading the poem itself. The inclusion of a puzzle became standard practice for Dodgson when writing his child-friends. He published the poem under the title "Lines. [Addressed to three little girls, with a copy of 'Holiday House.']" in his 1869 collection *Phantasmagoria.*

CATHERINE SINCLAIR (1800–64) wrote several novels as well as other works on such varied topics as women's education and Roman history. Dodgson must have felt an affinity for her work, as her approach to writing for children described in the preface could well refer to Dodgson's own goals in writing *Alice's Adventures in Wonderland:* "It was a remark of Sir Walter Scott's many years ago, to the author herself, that in the rising generation there would be no poets, wits, or orators, because all play of the imagination is now carefully discouraged, and books written for young persons are generally a mere dry record of facts, unenlivened by any appeal to the heart, or any excitement to the fancy."

8 LETTER

Charles L. Dodgson to Robinson Duckworth

Not dated, presumably Christ Church, Oxford

Dear Duckworth,
    Could you help to row my friends on Wednesday?
            Truly yours, *C.L. Dodgson*

WHETHER THIS particular boat trip took place is not clear, as the note bears no date. Robinson Duckworth (1834–1911) became a Fellow of Trinity College in 1860. He accompanied Dodgson and the Liddells on at least three boating parties over the next few years, often entertaining them by singing. Alice Liddell recalled that the "party usually consisted of five—one of Mr. Dodgson's men friends as well as himself and us three. His brother occasionally took an oar in the merry party, but our most usual fifth was Mr. Duckworth, who sang well."[1] In *Alice's Adventures in Wonderland,* Duckworth becomes the Duck, Dodgson the Dodo, Lorina the Lory, and Edith the Eaglet.

DODGSON RECORDED the now-famous boat trip in his diary: "Duckworth and I made an expedition *up* the river to Godstow with the three Liddells: we had tea on the bank there, and did not reach Ch[rist] Ch[urch] again till quarter past eight, when we took them on to my rooms to see my collection of microphotographs, and restored them to the Deanery just before nine."[2] Curiously, Dodgson did not "mark this day with a white stone" as he customarily did in his diary for special days. He did, however, annotate this entry a few months later, "On which occasion I told them the fairy-tale of "Alice's Adventures Under Ground," which I undertook to write out for Alice, and which is now finished (as to the text) though the pictures are not yet nearly done. Feb. 10, 1863."[3] Dodgson's words suggest that at that time the "fairy-tale" held significance for him only in relation to Alice Liddell.

DUCKWORTH GAVE his own account of the memorable expedition:

> I was very closely associated with him in the production and publication of 'Alice in Wonderland.' I rowed *stroke* and he rowed *bow* in the famous Long Vacation voyage to Godstow; when the three Miss Liddells were our passengers, and the story was actually composed and spoken *over my shoulder* for the benefit of Alice Liddell, who was acting as 'cox' of our gig. I remember turning round and saying, 'Dodgson, is this an extempore romance of yours?' And he replied, 'Yes, I'm inventing as we go along.' I also well remember how, when we had conducted the three children back to the Deanery, Alice said, as she bade us good-night, 'Oh, Mr Dodgson, I wish you would write out Alice's adventures for me.' He said he should try, and he afterwards told me that he sat up nearly the whole night, committing to a MS. book his recollections of the drolleries with which he had enlivened the afternoon. He added illustrations of his own, and presented the volume, which used often to be seen on the drawing-room table at the Deanery.[4]

1. Hargreaves, "Alice's Recollections of Carrollian Days," pp. 1–12.
2. Edward Wakeling, ed. *Lewis Carroll's Diaries: the private journals of Charles Lutwidge Dodgson*, (Luton, 1997), vol. iv, pp. 94–95.
3. Wakeling, *Lewis Carroll's Diaries*, vol. iv, p. 95.
4. Quoted in Stuart Dodgson Collingwood, ed. *The Lewis Carroll Picture Book*, (London, 1899), pp. 358–60. For accounts from Dodgson and Alice Liddell, see Lewis Carroll, "Alice on Stage" in Collingwood, *The Lewis Carroll Picture Book* and Hargreaves, "Alice's Recollections of Carrollian Days."

9 LETTER

Charles L. Dodgson to Robinson Duckworth

12 April 1864, Christ Church, Oxford
See illustration overleaf

Dear Duckworth,

Will you dine with me in Hall on Thursday? or on Saturday? And should you be disposed any day soon for a row on the river, for which I could procure some Liddells as companions.

Ever truly yours,
CL Dodgson

THIS SECOND boating invitation came almost two years after the famous expedition. Dodgson had already completed the text to "Alice," which he planned to give to Alice Liddell, but was still laboring over his own illustrations. At the same time, however, Dodgson had contracted with Macmillan and Company to publish the tale and commissioned John Tenniel, a leading illustrator and political cartoonist, to provide the illustrations.

DESPITE THE INVITATION, neither this nor any more boat trips with the Liddells took place. Some nine months earlier, a rift had developed between Dodgson and the Liddells that has never been fully explained. Dodgson's diary for 1863 survives, but the page presumably chronicling the break has been excised. A later note written in Dodgson's niece's hand summarizes at least part of the contents of that page: "L. C. learns from Mrs. Liddell that he is supposed to be using the children as a means of paying court to the governess. He is also supposed by some to be courting Ina."[1] The Liddells left Oxford for the summer a few days after the date of the missing entry. When they returned in the autumn, Dodgson noted, "Mrs. Liddell and the children were there, but I held aloof from them, as I have done all this term."[2] There was a brief reunion later, but visits with the Liddells gradually ceased.

THIS LETTER demonstrates that the impetus to end the friendship had come from Mrs. Liddell. Dodgson recorded on May 12, 1864: "During these last few days I have applied in vain for leave to take the children on the river, i.e. Alice, Edith, and Rhoda ⌈the next youngest sister, age five⌉: but Mrs. Liddell will not let *any* come in future—rather superfluous caution."[3] Probably taking his cue from the rumors of the year before, Dodgson assumed that Lorina, by then fifteen, would have been considered too old to accompany him without a chaperone. The newfound coolness may also have stemmed from other causes: Dodgson's biographers have long supposed that Mrs. Liddell was disturbed by Dodgson's love for Alice. There is also speculation that Dodgson may have suggested an eventual marriage between himself and Alice, a match that would have earned Mrs. Liddell's disapproval.[4]

1. Wakeling, *Lewis Carroll's Diaries*, vol. iv, p. 214, fn. 227.
2. Wakeling, *Lewis Carroll's Diaries*, vol. iv, p. 264.
3. Wakeling, *Lewis Carroll's Diaries*, vol. iv, p. 229.
4. See Michael Bakewell, *Lewis Carroll: A Biography* (London, 1996), Morton N. Cohen, *Lewis Carroll: A Biography* (New York, 1995); Anne Clark, *Lewis Carroll: A Biography* (New York, 1979), and Derek Hudson, *Lewis Carroll: An Illustrated Biography* (London, rev. ed. 1976).

10 FACSIMILE

Charles L. Dodgson, *Alice's Adventures under Ground*

⌈Camden, New Jersey: privately printed facsimile of original 1864 manuscript for Eldridge R Johnson by Max Jaffe, Vienna, 1936⌉
Limp green morocco with gilt-stamped title

THE FIRST INCARNATION of *Alice's Adventures in Wonderland* was the hand-written and illustrated "Alice's Adventures under Ground." Dodgson took great pains fashioning this gift for Alice Liddell and did not

9. Charles L. Dodgson,
letter to Robinson Duckworth, 1864

complete the manuscript until well over a year after the famous boat trip. He presented it to Alice Liddell on November 26, 1864, by which time their friendship had cooled. The first page bears his decorated inscription, "A Christmas Gift to a Dear Child in Memory of a Summer Day." Although in the manuscript version of the story Dodgson did not specify the age of "Alice," in the published version, her age is seven. Alice Liddell was ten at the time of the story's invention, and she had turned twelve by the time she received the gift. Dodgson thus separated the heroine of his story from his special child-friend. The "Alice" of Dodgson's illustrations is not a representation of Alice Liddell with her distinctive chin-length bob and bangs. Yet on the last page, Dodgson melded his story heroine with her inspirational counterpart by pasting a photograph of Alice Liddell at age eight, taken during

the same July 1860 session as "Open your mouth, and bob for a cherry," a poignant reminder of Alice's growing up—and away from—Dodgson.[1] This facsimile was commissioned in the 1930s by Eldridge Johnson, who had just purchased the original manuscript from Dr. Rosenbach.

1. Underneath this photograph, Dodgson had drawn a picture of Alice Liddell, clearly copied from the photograph. Evidently dissatisfied with his drawing, Dodgson placed the photograph over it. The drawing itself remained unknown until Morton Cohen discovered it in 1977.

11 BOOKS

Lewis Carroll, *Alice's Adventures in Wonderland*

London: Macmillan and Co., 1866
Red cloth with gilt-stamped picture cover
Inscribed on half-title: "R. Duckworth | with the sincere regards of | the Author. | in memory of our voyage."

The Duck,
from the Dodo.

9. June. 1887.

ALICE'S ADVENTURES
UNDER GROUND.

1

11. Charles L. Dodgson,
inscription to Robinson Duckworth
in *Alice's Adventures under Ground*, 1887

Lewis Carroll, *Alice's Adventures under Ground*

London and New York: Macmillan and Co., 1886
Red cloth with gilt-stamped picture cover
Inscribed on half-title: "The Duck | from the Dodo. |
    9. June 1887."

DODGSON GAVE presentation copies of his books to his friends throughout his life, sometimes bound specially in white vellum or a particular color of morocco (goatskin). Dodgson's gift to Duckworth of an 1866 edition of *Alice's Adventures in Wonderland* had the regular red cloth binding, but the distinctive inscription commemorates Duckworth's participation in the memorable boat trip of 1862.

DODGSON'S INSCRIPTION to Duckworth twenty years later in *Alice's Adventures under Ground*, his published facsimile of the original manuscript, is more humorous. "The Duck from the Dodo" refers to Duckworth's and Dodgson's incarnations within the story. After Duckworth moved away from Oxford to take an appointment in the church, the two men lost close contact. This presentation copy testifies to their continued friendship and the role Duckworth had played in the beginnings of Dodgson's famous story.

"Some people declare that I am no humourist, that I have no sense of fun at all; they deny me everything but severity, 'classicality,' and dignity. Now, *I* believe that I have a very keen sense of humour, and that my drawings are sometimes really funny."

 —Sir John Tenniel, in M.H. Spielmann,
  "Sir John Tenniel," *The Magazine of Art* 1895

IN THE YEARS since the publication of *Alice,* Sir John Tenniel (1820–1914) has become almost as renowned for its creation as Dodgson. Tenniel's fame in this context obscures a long and successful career in other arenas of art. He worked as an illustrator for *Punch* beginning in 1850 and became its chief political cartoonist in 1862. He produced some two thousand cartoons and illustrated nearly three dozen books during his lifetime. These numbers bespeak both his popularity (Tenniel was knighted in 1893) and his long career—it was blindness that forced him to retire in 1901. Tenniel was thus an established artist when Dodgson, then a young and unknown Oxford don, approached him in 1864 to illustrate his "fairy-tale."

DODGSON AT FIRST planned to illustrate *Alice* himself, but due to artistic limitations that he readily admitted, he sought an introduction to Tenniel through a mutual friend at *Punch*. Tenniel agreed to the project and, by the spring of 1865, he had completed the forty-two drawings to be engraved on wood for the book. Similarities between Dodgson's and Tenniel's illustrations suggest that Tenniel must have seen either Dodgson's preliminary sketches or the manuscript itself before Dodgson gave it to Alice Liddell. No correspondence from Dodgson to Tenniel is known to survive, but Tenniel probably received constant instructions from the detail-minded author, who had commissioned the artist himself under the terms of his publishing contract. Dodgson, however, held Tenniel in great esteem for his high standard of perfection. It was Tenniel, citing sloppy typography and poor reproductions of his work, who urged Dodgson to scuttle the first printing of *Alice's Adventures in Wonderland.*

DODGSON WAS EAGER to avail himself of Tenniel's services once again when he began working on *Through the Looking-Glass* in 1866. Tenniel, busy with the demands of *Punch*, agreed in 1868 to execute the drawings in his spare time, but the book did not appear for another three years. Dodgson eventually resigned himself to the delay in order to have the desired illustrations. When Dodgson asked Tenniel to illustrate a subsequent book, the artist claimed he would not undertake woodcut illustrations anymore. Tenniel worked in pencil and produced drawings with subtle, soft lines that were difficult to translate into the hard lines of a wood engraving for publication. Dodgson was forced to turn to several other illustrators, but continued to hold up Tenniel as his ideal.

12 DRAWINGS

John Tenniel, Five final drawings for *Alice's Adventures in Wonderland*
1865. Pencil on paper

FIVE of Tenniel's original illustrations for *Alice's Adventures in Wonderland* are preserved at the Rosenbach. They were added to Dodgson's own copy of the rare first edition of *Alice* when it was rebound by a later owner, Stuart M. Samuel, in 1899. The delicate pencil drawings have since been removed from the book to prevent abrasion and also enable their simultaneous exhibition. These are not preliminary sketches—some of which do survive for *Looking-Glass*—but the final drawings from which the Dalziel brothers worked up their wood engravings for publication. Tenniel was never fully satisfied with these reproductive prints, which despite their quality transform his soft contours into precise, clear lines and his subtle, shimmering passages into strong fields of black and white. Even today, the drawings are difficult to reproduce photographically without distortion.

"THE WHITE RABBIT" is the first text illustration to *Alice,* and a harbinger—a rabbit on its hind legs pulls a pocket watch from its waistcoat—of the nonsense to come. The book's second illustration is "A LITTLE DOOR ABOUT FIFTEEN INCHES HIGH," and is the first appearance of Alice. Two further—and likely later—drawings by Tenniel for the scene survive at Harvard University. In "THE POOL OF TEARS," the now shrunken Alice swims in a sea of her own tears, both chasing after the mouse and scaring him away with constant talk of cats and dogs. When she promises not to torment him anymore, he agrees to relate "THE MOUSE'S TALE." With the eaglet, the lory and many other animals gathered around him, drying off from the salt-water bath, the mouse begins a rather discursive history of England. The dodo soon moves to end the tale by suggesting a race.

12. John Tenniel, "The Mouse's Tale," pencil drawing, 1865

"What Will Become of Me?" brings us to the White Rabbit's house, where Alice has assumed gargantuan proportions from eating little cakes; she ". . . put one arm out of the window and one foot up the chimney." This drawing, more than any other by Tenniel, follows closely the model provided by Dodgson's own sketch in the original manuscript.

13 DRAWINGS

John Tenniel, Four final drawings for *Through the Looking-Glass*

1871. Pencil and white heightening on paper
See illustrations on outside wrapper

IN CONTRAST to the technique earlier used for the final drawings in *Alice's Adventures in Wonderland*, Tenniel employed pencil, pen and white heightening together on the final drawings for *Looking-Glass*. The altered technique anticipates the inevitable transformation of the subtle drawings into pure line for reproduction as wood engravings in the printed book. The Rosenbach Museum & Library preserves 26 final drawings for *Looking-Glass*; these may be compared with preliminary sketches and tracings for transfer now in a private collection (see below).

THE DOUBLE-SIDED DRAWING "Through the Looking-glass" epitomizes the brilliant results of the partnership between Tenniel and Dodgson, though Dodgson at first rejected the idea of two images for the scene (see Dodgson's April 15, 1870 letter to Macmillan, cited in the following section). The drawing on the recto depicts Alice's discovery that the mantelpiece mirror was ". . . beginning to melt away, just like a bright silvery mist." Tenniel's drawing is so subtly executed as to mimic the silvery mist. On the verso, Alice has quite literally come through the looking-glass to find a similar and yet profoundly different world. The now-smiling clock-face is but one example. Properly speaking, the recto is a sketch for which another version also exists (illustrated on back cover); the verso (Alice emerging) is the actual final drawing. Alice encounters "THE WHITE KING" immediately upon her descent from the mantelpiece. She helps the blustery little king to regain his position at the table. Much further on in the book, "TWEEDLEDUM TEARS HIS HAIR" when he discovers his rattle has been ruined. "YOU MAY SHAKE HANDS" is the classic scene of Humpty-Dumpty offering his hand to Alice.

14 BOOK

Lewis Carroll, *Through the Looking-Glass, and what Alice found there*

London: Macmillan and Company, 1872, containing preliminary sketches and autograph tracings for transfer by John Tenniel
Red cloth with gilt-stamped picture cover. Private collection

AS WITH the above volumes, a later bibliophile rebound this first-edition *Looking-Glass* with numerous drawings by John Tenniel. Interleaved next to the printed illustrations, the thirty-eight works include both preliminary sketches and tracings for transfer. Tenniel produced the tracings, with their simple and strong contours, to be used as transfer guides for the wood-engravers, who had difficulty working from his subtle drawings.

15 LETTER

John Tenniel to Edmund Evans

9 August 1883, Maida Hill, London

My dear Sir,

A week or so ago Mr. Dodgson wrote to say that he is "quite satisfied" with your estimate. I should have told you this sooner, but have been away in the country.

I shall be very glad if you will get on with the "enlargements" as soon as possible. Mr. Dodgson is very anxious about it, and so am I. Of course the smaller pictures must be in the same *proportion* to the size of the page as the larger ones, and equally of course I must see *all* the photographed blocks, before engraving, as they will probably require re-touching apart from the actual "alteration" in the dress etc etc.

When do you think you will be able to make a beginning? If you should wish to see me on the subject I am *always* at home in the morning.

Yours faithfully
John Tenniel

THE ROSENBACH preserves five letters written by Sir John Tenniel to Edmund Evans, the noted color wood-engraver, regarding the printing of his illustrations for *The Nursery "Alice,"* a later version of *Alice's Adventures in Wonderland* (see next section). Just as Dodgson carefully watched over the details in the process of publishing his books, Tenniel showed great concern over the printing of his illustrations.

16. John and Charles Watkins,
photograph of John Tenniel, not dated

16 PHOTOGRAPH

John and Charles Watkins, Portrait of John Tenniel

Not dated. Albumen print

IN THIS typical professional studio photograph, Tenniel—in a pose of ease and confidence—appears with books and a classical-style bust at an elaborately ornamented table. The pairing of a gentleman with such accoutrements of education and a dramatic drape was a formula quickly established by nineteenth-century photographers, based on the tradition of painted portraiture. Although Dodgson photographed himself as an educated gentleman, he never chose a photographic studio with elaborate backdrops. Dodgson's face almost always appears in at least partial profile, in contrast to this image of Tenniel.

Alice in Print: Macmillan and Company

"From Messrs. Macmillan and Co. comes a glorious artistic treasure, a book to put on one's shelf as an antidote to a fit of the blues; "Alice's Adventures in Wonderland," by Lewis Carroll, with forty-two illustrations by John Tenniel, sure to be run after as one of the most popular works of its class."

—*The Reader*, November 18, 1865

ONCE Dodgson had completed the text of "Alice's Adventures under Ground," he shared it with some of his friends. Fellow author of children's books George MacDonald encouraged him to seek a publisher for his "fairy tale," which Dodgson found in the up-and-coming firm of Macmillan and Company. Self-taught intellectuals, Scottish brothers Alexander and Daniel Macmillan came from a poor family, but had worked their way up in the bookselling profession to purchase their own shop in Cambridge. There they established an informal meeting-place for an intellectual community that included novelists William Makepeace Thackeray and Charles Kingsley. Still a young firm in the 1860s, Macmillan had already achieved considerable success with authors such as Kingsley and Thomas Hughes. They relocated to London in 1863, the year in which Dodgson and Alexander Macmillan first met. The correspondence between Dodgson and Macmillan and Company is voluminous: over 450 letters from Dodgson to Macmillan are preserved in the Rosenbach collections.[1] A very small selection is here interspersed with the *Alice* books.

MACMILLAN and Company published *Alice's Adventures in Wonderland*, and all of Dodgson's subsequent books, on commission. In nineteenth-century publishing, this was not an unusual arrangement. Dodgson thus paid all of the production expenses, including the cost of materials, fees for illustrations, even advertising. Macmillan and Company oversaw the production and distribution of each book, for which it received a percentage of the net profit. The arrangement made Dodgson bear most of the risk but also gave him almost complete control over the quality, price, and look of his books. It also allowed him to make demands of his publishers that seem surprising today, particularly given that Dodgson was an unknown mathematics lecturer in the early 1860s. But Dodgson looked to Alexander Macmillan for advice, sending him scores of questions in addition to instructions. Macmillan patiently opined on advertising strategies, bindings, prices, ideas for new books both by Dodgson and his

friends, relations with booksellers, profits, and so on. The firm constantly sent him specially bound copies of his books in response to his requests. Dodgson occasionally asked the firm to purchase theater tickets for him, or track down addresses of child-actors to whom he wished to present copies of *Alice*, and once to retrieve his pocket watch from an errant repairman.

1. See Morton N. Cohen and Anita Gandolfo, *Lewis Carroll and the House of Macmillan* (Cambridge, 1987). The book prints the majority of Dodgson's letters to Macmillan and provides a more detailed description of the relationship between Dodgson and Macmillan.

17 BOOK

Lewis Carroll, *Alice's Adventures in Wonderland*

London: Macmillan and Co., 1865
White vellum binding with gilt-stamped decoration articulated by red painted flowers
Inscribed in black ink on first fly-leaf:

> To M.A.B.
> The Royal MAB, dethroned, discrowned
>   By rebel fairies wild,
> Has found a home on English ground,
>   And lives an English child.
> I know it, Maiden, when I see
> A fairy-tale upon your knee,
> And note the page that idly lingers
> Beneath those still and listless fingers,
> And mark those dreamy looks that stray
> To brighter visions far away,
> Still seeking in the pictured story
> The memory of a vanished glory.

THE FIRST EDITION of *Alice's Adventures in Wonderland* has become famous in the annals of book production and is one of the most highly sought-after of rare books. Dodgson commissioned an initial print run of 2,000 at the Clarendon Press in Oxford. Fifty of these had already been bound, with the date 1865 on the title-page, and given away as presentation copies, when Tenniel wrote to Dodgson expressing dismay about the quality of the printing. In response, Dodgson decided to replace the 2,000 with a new set prepared by a different printer, Richard Clay of London, at considerable expense to himself.

AT HIS REQUEST, most of Dodgson's friends returned their copies and later received the new printing, dated 1866. Dodgson donated many of the re-

To M.A.B.

The royal MAB, dethroned, discrowned
    By rebel fairies wild,
Has found a home on English ground,
    And lives an English child.
I know it, Maiden, when I see
A fairy-tale upon your knee,
And note the page that idly lingers
Beneath those still and listless fingers,
And mark those dreamy looks that stray
To brighter visions far away,
Still seeking in the pictured story
The memory of a vanished glory.

17. Charles L. Dodgson, inscription to Mary Ann Bessy Terry
in *Alice's Adventures in Wonderland*, 1865

turned copies to hospitals and homes. A total of twenty-two copies are known to survive today. Most have found their way from great American private collections into public institutions.

THE Rosenbach "1865 *Alice*" is a fittingly precious copy. It was first presented to the child-actress Marion Terry (1853–1930), of the famous acting family in whose acquaintance Dodgson took much pride. The dedicatory poem "To M.A.B." inscribed on the flyleaf alludes to both "Mary Ann Bessy," her given name, and the mythical fairy Queen Mab. Like most of Dodgson's friends, Terry must have returned this copy upon Dodgson's request, and it remained in his possession until his death. Stuart M. Samuel acquired the book from the Dodgson estate and had it rebound with proofs of Tenniel's woodcuts (also purchased from the sale) and five pencil drawings purchased directly from Tenniel. The Tenniel proofs and drawings have now been matted separately to ensure their conservation.[1] The 1899 Riviere and Son binding is white vellum with the usual circular medallions of Alice with the pig and the Cheshire cat gilt-stamped on either side, with red roses, sprays of leaves, and gold bees added.

1. See Justin Schiller and Selwyn H. Goodacre, *Alice's Adventures in Wonderland: An 1865 printing re-described* (Privately printed, 1990), pp. 38–40, for a more detailed description of the history of this book.

18 LETTER

Charles L. Dodgson to Alexander Macmillan

24 May 1865, Christ Church, Oxford

Dear Sir,

Thanks for the specimen volume. I like the look of it exceedingly. 3 alterations I should like made.

(1) The title is incomplete: it should be

ALICE'S
ADVENTURES IN
WONDERLAND

(2) I should like gold lines round the cat side as well as the other. I want the 2 sides to look equally ornamental.

(3) This I am rather doubtful about—but I don't quite like the look of gilt-edges at one end. As I want it to be a *table*-book, I fancy it would look better with the edges evenly cut smooth, and no gilding.

We hope to begin working off on Monday. My present idea is, to send you 50 copies to be bound first, for me to give away to friends, and the rest of the 2000 you can bind at your leisure and publish at whatever time of the year you think best—but for my own

young friends I want copies as soon as possible: they are all growing out of childhood so alarmingly fast.

One of the 50 I should like bound in white vellum: the rest in red like the specimen.

Believe me
truly yours,
C. L. Dodgson

DODGSON had chosen red over green in a previous letter, and 'Alice red' became his favorite color for the bindings of his children's books. Always one to fuss over detail, Dodgson often pinpointed the tiniest mistakes for corrections. He insisted on the highest possible quality—within a reasonable amount of expenditure—for his books and deliberated carefully over their aesthetic aspects. *Alice's Adventures in Wonderland* subsequently appeared with gilt edges.

THIRTEEN-YEAR-OLD Alice Liddell received the white vellum-bound copy on July 4, 1865, the anniversary of the original river excursion. When Dodgson recalled the first edition, he exchanged Alice's copy for the second printing, which was sent to her on December 14, 1865. This copy, however, was bound in dark blue morocco. Dodgson, an inveterate royal lion-hunter, instead sent a white vellum-bound copy to Princess Beatrice, Queen Victoria's youngest daughter.[1]

1. Dodgson recorded these facts on a blank page in his diary in a list of dates concerning *Alice's Adventures in Wonderland*. See Appendix B in Roger Lancelyn Green, *The Diaries of Lewis Carroll*, (New York and Oxford, 1954), p. 554.

19 BOOK

Lewis Carroll, *Alice's Adventures in Wonderland*

New York: D. Appleton and Co., 1866
Red cloth with gilt-stamped picture cover

AFTER Dodgson decided to print a new set of 2,000 copies and recall the fifty that had already been bound and given to friends, he was left with 1,950 remaindered sets. The Dodgson–Macmillan correspondence demonstrates that after some deliberation these were sold to the Appleton firm of New York. Appleton bound the 'new' book in the same red cloth with gilt-stamped medallions of Alice and the Cheshire Cat, but stamped the name Appleton on the spine rather than Macmillan. Appleton also printed a title-page with its own name and the date 1866. This American binding of the suppressed first edition has become a sought-after rare book.

20 LETTER

Charles L. Dodgson to Alexander Macmillan

31 July 1865, Croft Rectory, Darlington

Dear Sir,

Thanks for your letter with its alarming estimate—£100 more than it cost to print the book in Oxford. I rather doubt the wisdom of incurring such a large additional expense, but would like answers to the following questions:—

(1) What would be the cost of printing *1000*, instead of 2000?

(2) Would Mr. Clay print from the electro-types (as I should certainly prefer)?

(3) In case we have the first edition so printed, what should you advise me to do with regard to the 2000 printed at Oxford? The choice seems to lie between these courses:—

(a) reserve them till next year, "to sell in the provinces" (as has been suggested to me), or to send abroad, but keeping the price to 7s. 6d.

(b) sell them at a reduced price (say 5s.) as being avowedly an inferior edition, stating in the advertisement what the two editions differ in.

(c) get Mr. Clay, or some experienced man, to look them over, and select all such sheets as happen to be well printed—use these along with the London-printed copies, and sell the rest as waste paper.

(d) sell the whole as waste paper.

In case (a) I should of course pay Mr. Combe's bill in full. In the other cases we should of course have to come to some other agreement.

Of these 4 courses, (a) seems to me scarcely honest, and my own opinion inclines to (d). However I should like to know what you think about it.

> Believe me
> very truly yours,
> *C. L. Dodgson*

DODGSON'S WORRIES about the expense of a second printing are hardly surprising given that he would have to pay it out of his fairly limited income from Christ Church. His decision to reprint the book demonstrates his absolute unwillingness to compromise his standards: he calculated in his diary that he could not possibly make a profit on the sale of the book unless it went into a second printing. Despite his hesitancy "to sell in the provinces," that was of course the solution eventually adopted at the suggestion of Macmillan with the sale of the first printing to the American firm of Appleton.

21 BOOK

Lewis Carroll, *Alice's Adventures in Wonderland*

London: Macmillan and Co., 1866
Red cloth with gilt-stamped picture cover
Inscribed on half-title: "Dymphna Ellis, | from the Author"

THE SECOND printing by Richard Clay was issued in England as the new first edition. Dated 1866, it was actually issued in the fall of 1865 to catch the crucial Christmas trade when book sales were most vigorous. Dodgson recorded that he "received from Macmillan a copy of the new impression of *Alice*—very *far* superior to the old, and in fact a perfect piece of artistic printing."[1] The book received almost uniform praise from the critics, and within a year was in its fifth thousand. Dymphna Ellis (1854–1930), the daughter of fellow amateur photographer the Vicar of Cranbourne, was a child-friend and photographic subject in the 1860s.

1. Green, *The Diaries of Lewis Carroll*, p. 236.

22 BOOK

Lewis Carroll, *Through the Looking-glass and what Alice found there*

London: Macmillan and Co., 1872
Red cloth with gilt-stamped picture cover
Inscribed on half-title: "Presented to | J. Ruskin | by the Author | Nov. 19. 1875"

DODGSON FIRST mentioned his plan to write a sequel to *Alice* in an August 24, 1866 letter to Macmillan: "It will be some time before I again indulge in paper and print. I have, however, a floating idea of writing a sort of sequel to *Alice*, and if it ever comes to anything, I intend to consult you at the very outset, so as to have the thing properly managed from the beginning." The book did not appear for another five years, until December 1871 (dated 1872). This copy was presented to John Ruskin, the foremost art critic of the time and the first Slade Professor of Art at Oxford. Ruskin, also a notorious admirer of children, had a sporadic friendship with Dodgson, who photographed him in 1875. From time to time, Dodgson asked Ruskin's opinion on the skill of illustrators or artistic friends. Ruskin also gave drawing lessons to Alice Liddell, who was a talented watercolorist.

23 LETTER

Charles L. Dodgson to Alexander Macmillan

15 April 1870, Christ Church, Oxford

Dear Mr. Macmillan,

My title-page [for *Through the Looking-Glass*] hasn't had fair play yet—as the printer doesn't follow out my directions. I want the large capitals to have *more below the line than above:* nearly twice as much. In the corrected copy I send the A and F have slipped a little lower than I meant: the others are about right.

Secondly, the "AND" ought to be half-way between the two lines, and not (as they have printed it) nearer to the upper line.

Thirdly, the 3 lines of title ought to be closer together, and not so close to the top of the page.

Fourthly, the comma and full-stop ought to be set lower.

All of the above faults I have endeavoured to remedy in the corrected copy I enclose.

I send an uncorrected one with it that you may see the difference.

As to the picture-title you suggested, I forgot to tell you a circumstance which puts an end to the idea at once. Mr. Tenniel has drawn a picture of the looking-glass, with Alice getting through it, to come in at page 11. It will not do to have two different pictures of the same thing.

I am sorry you have given any more thought to the 'copyright' subject. My curiosity is quite satisfied, and (as I said before) I have not the least idea of really selling it.

I will ask my Italian friend (Signor T. Pietrocòla Rossetti) if he can give any advice about a publisher.

His own translation of his cousin's *Goblin Market* is printed (and I suppose published) at Firenze. But can't *you* manage that part of the business? Is there no great publisher at Rome you could apply to?

  Very truly yours,
   C.L. Dodgson

P.S. I have finally abandoned the idea that alarmed you so much, of petitioning for photographs.

I want to have the presentation-copy of the 'Looking Glass' (I mean the one for Miss A. Liddell) bound with an oval piece of looking-glass let into the cover. Will you consult your binder as to whether the thing is practicable? It should not be larger, I think, in proportion to the book, than I have here drawn it.

THIS LETTER typifies the kind of detailed instructions Macmillan frequently received from Dodgson. Macmillan did publish an Italian translation of *Alice*, executed by T. Pietròcola Rossetti, a cousin of the Pre-Raphaelite artist Dante Gabriel Rossetti and his sister, poet Christina Rossetti. Macmillan had earlier published Christina Rossetti's *Goblin Market*.

EVER IN SEARCH of images of beautiful children, Dodgson evidently suggested that Macmillan place a request in the next edition of *Alice* for child-readers to send carte-de-visite photographs to him care of the publisher. Dodgson agrees to forego the idea in the postscript of this letter after Macmillan had replied in horror at the thought, explaining in an unusually humorous vein,

Did you ever take a Shower Bath? Or do you remember your first? To appeal to all your young admirers for their photograph! If your Shower Bath were filled a-top with bricks instead of water it would be about the fate you court! But if you will do it, there is no help for it, and as in duty bound we will help you to the self-immolation. Cartes! I should think so, in-deed—cart loads of them. Think of the postmen. Open an office for relief at the North Pole and another at the Equator. Ask President Grant, the Emperor of China, the Governor General of India, the whatever do you call him of Melbourne, if they won't help you. But it's no use remonstrating with you. But I am resigned. I return from Scotland next Monday a week. I shall be braced for encountering this awful idea.[1]

AT THE TIME of the publication of *Through the Looking-glass*, Alice Liddell was nineteen, and Dodgson had had little contact with his former child-muse for some years. The request to include a tiny mirror in the binding of a special presentation copy to her did not bear fruit either. Dodgson gave Alice a copy bound in red morocco.

1. Quoted in Cohen and Gandolfo, *Lewis Carroll and the House of Macmillan,* p. 85.

24 BOOK

Lewis Carroll, *Alice's Adventures under Ground*

London and New York: Macmillan and Co., 1886
Red cloth with gilt-stamped picture cover

DODGSON FIRST SUGGESTED publishing a facsimile of his original manuscript to Macmillan in a letter on March 22, 1885:

I have a project to submit to you, for a fresh venture in publication, which I hope will meet with your approval. For myself it will probably prove a considerable loss, as I expect the cost of production will be enormous: but it will at any rate put an honest penny into *your* pocket! My idea is to publish, in facsimile, the original MS book of *Alice's Adventures*, which was done in printing-hand, with pen-and-ink drawings of my own.

Ch. Ch. Ap. 15. 1870

Dear Mr. Macmillan,

My title-page hasn't had fair play yet — as the printer doesn't follow out my directions. I want the large capitals to have more below the line than above: nearly twice as much. In the "corrected" copy I send the A & F have slipped a little lower than I meant: the others are about right.

Secondly, the 'AND' ought to be half-way between the two lines, and not (as they have printed it) nearer to the upper line —

Thirdly, the 3 lines of

P.S. I have finally abandoned the idea that alarmed you so much, of petitioning for photo-graphs ——

I want to have the presentation-copy of the "Looking-glass" (I mean the one for Miss A. Liddell) bound with an oval piece of looking-glass let into the cover. Will you consult your binder as to whether the thing is practicable? It should not be larger, I think, in proportion to the book, than I have here drawn it.

Rev C L Dodgson

23. Charles L. Dodgson, letter to Alexander Macmillan, 1870

DODGSON HAD ALREADY written to Alice Liddell, by then Mrs. Hargreaves, to request the loan of the manuscript and permission to publish it. She granted permission, apparently with the stipulation that the photograph of herself on the last page not be reproduced. Dodgson concurred in a letter to her—"My own wishes would be distinctly *against* reproducing the photograph"[1]—and the photograph was covered by a piece of paper reading "THE END," in a gesture that resonates symbolically as well as literally. Dodgson insisted that the manuscript not leave his hands during publication, and so a photographer was dispatched to Oxford to photograph the pages in Dodgson's presence.

1. Letter from Charles L. Dodgson to Alice Hargreaves, 7 March 1885, Rosenbach Museum & Library.

25 LETTER

Charles L. Dodgson to Alexander Macmillan

13 September 1886, Eastbourne

Dear Mr. Macmillan,

Would you kindly send this note by a messenger? Mrs. Carlo has moved to the opposite side of the street, but I do not know the number, so can think of no other way of reaching her than sending it by hand.

Have you any ideas as to the cover of *Alice's Adventures Under Ground?* The book will be about the thickness of the *Snark.* I assume that it must be red cloth and gilt edges, to match the other *Alices.* But we cannot have medallions: my drawings are too bad for that. So *my* idea is to have the title printed in gold, in some fanciful way, on one side, no gold lines, and the back and the other side left without device.

If you approve the idea, can you find an artist to design a good title?

Very truly yours,
C. L. Dodgson

DODGSON ADOPTED the design he included in this letter for the 'Alice red' binding of the book. His request that Macmillan and Company deliver a note to Mrs. Carlo—the mother of Phoebe Carlo, the first actress to play Alice on the London stage—is again typical of Dodgson.

26 BOOK

Lewis Carroll, *The Nursery "Alice" containing twenty coloured enlargements from Tenniel's illustrations to "Alice's Adventures in Wonderland" with text adapted to nursery readers by Lewis Carroll*

London: Macmillan and Co., 1890
White boards, both illustrated in printed color
Inscribed on half-title: "Miss C. Rossetti, | with the Author's Sincere regards. | Mar. 25. 1890."

DODGSON'S LAST INCARNATION of *Alice* is a simplified retelling of the tale for children from "Nought to Five" with twenty of the original illustrations colored by Tenniel and enlarged. Emily Gertrude Thomson (1850–1929), a friend of Dodgson who specialized in fairy drawings, executed the cover image, based loosely on Tenniel's drawings. She also illustrated Dodgson's last book, a collection of poems, with drawings of child-like fairies.

AS USUAL, desiring to provide the best quality available, Dodgson had the illustrations for *The Nursery "Alice"* engraved by Edmund Evans, the premier color wood-engraver of the time. Evans was at the forefront of the development of high quality colored picture-books for children in the 1870s and 1880s, with the works of Kate Greenaway, Walter Crane, and Randolph Caldecott. Although so many children's books of the time contained color pictures, *The Nursery "Alice"* was Dodgson's only large-scale picture-book.

DODGSON MADE a marked departure from *Alice's Adventures in Wonderland* in the text of *The Nursery "Alice."* A series of questions lead the child-reader through the process of reading and looking at the pictures. There are comments about the illustrations, including their color, and reassurances that pictures of various characters will appear later in the narrative. Dodgson encourages the child to interact with the book physically: in regard to the White Rabbit's nervousness at the beginning of the story, he includes the parenthesis "(Don't you see how he's trembling? Just shake the book a little, from side to side, and you'll soon see him tremble)." Or, when Alice falls into the Pool of Tears, he asks "Doesn't Alice look pretty, as she swims across the picture? You can just see her blue stockings, far away under the water." In the preface "addressed to any mother," Dodgson opines the book is not to be read, but "rather to be thumbed, to be cooed over, to be dogs'-eared, to be rumpled, to be kissed, by the illiterate, ungrammatical, dimpled Darlings, that fill your Nursery with merry uproar, and your inmost heart of hearts with a restful gladness!"

DODGSON PRESENTED this copy to poet Christina Rossetti, whom he had met and photographed in the 1860s. She published her own children's book, *Speaking Likenesses,* modeled on *Alice.*[1]

1. See U.C. Knoepflmacher, "Avenging Alice: Christina Rossetti and Lewis Carroll," *Nineteenth-Century Literature* (1986), pp. 299–328.

gilt edges, to match the other "Alices". But we cannot have medallions: my drawings are too bad for that — So my idea is to have the title printed in gold, in some fanciful way, on one side, no gold lines, & the back & the other side left without device.

If you approve the idea, can you find an artist to design a good title?

Very truly yours,
C. L. Dodgson

25. Charles L. Dodgson, letter to Alexander Macmillan, 1886

Memorandum of Agreement

Dated *18th November 1885*

BETWEEN

Revd C. L. Dodgson

AND

MACMILLAN & CO.

FOR THE PUBLICATION OF

"A Tangled Tale"

Terms:– Account to Author at 3/3 each for copies sold, he paying all expenses.

28. Memorandum of Agreement between Charles L. Dodgson and Macmillan & Co., 1885

27 LETTER

Charles L. Dodgson to Alexander Macmillan

23 June 1889, Christ Church, Oxford

Dear Mr. Macmillan,

(1) Will you kindly get me 2 stalls (front or 2nd row) for *Little Lord Fauntleroy* at the Opéra Comique for Wednesday afternoon the 26th: and leave them at Mr. Wells, 431. Strand.: and let me know you have done so?

(2) Please *stop* the binding of the 2 coloured Nursery *"Alice"* in morocco: and substitute 2 of those done in *brown* ink only.

(3) The other 4, in brown ink only are to be covered in covers, done in brown ink only, which Mr. Evans will send you.

(4) The 2 copies, with *colour*, and without covers, to be sent to me at Oxford.

(5) The leatherette copies of *Alice Under Ground* have arrived. Thanks.

(6) It is a great disappointment to me to have to postpone, till Xmas, the publication of the *Nursery "Alice"*, but it is absolutely necessary. The pictures are *far* too bright and gaudy, and vulgarise the whole thing. *None must be sold in England:* to do so would be to sacrifice whatever reputation I now have for giving the public the *best* I can. Mr. Evans must begin again, and print 10,000 *with Tenniel's coloured pictures before him:* and I must *see* all the proofs this time: and then we shall have a book really fit to offer to the public.

(7) As to the 10,000 already printed, I want you (as soon as you get the covers, and the 1000 special title-pages and 'list of works' prepared for America) to cover 500, and send them out, and see if they will buy the lot. The present arrangement is, you know, that you are to account to me, for all copies sold (whether here or in America) at 2s.3d. each: but, if you can sell *the whole 10,000* in America (which would be £1125), I am willing to knock off the £125.

Very truly yours,
C. L. Dodgson

P.S. The picture at p 44 is enough, by itself, to spoil the whole book!

"THE NURSERY 'ALICE,'" like its predecessors, has a colorful publishing history. Intended to appear in 1889, Dodgson initially had an ambitious 10,000 copies printed. However, due to problems with the illustrations, Dodgson was once again displeased. He felt Edmund Evans had printed the colors too brightly and decided the entire 10,000 should be reprinted. Evans did indeed reprint the book, even re-engraving some of the color blocks. It was the actual second printing, with more refined colors on whiter paper, that was sold in England as the first edition, dated 1890. 4,000 copies of the first, botched printing were purchased by an American publisher and sold in America, where evidently readers were thought less discerning. They bear the date 1890, but indicate New York rather than London on the title-page. Of the remaining 6,000, one hundred were sent to Australia and 5,900 were issued as a cheaper "People's Edition" in 1891. Sales were not as successful as hoped. Eventually the People's Edition was withdrawn from sale, and Dodgson donated the remainder to hospitals and homes for children.

THE LETTER also refers to a few copies that Dodgson had had printed with the illustrations in brown ink rather than in full color in order to be able to give promised copies to friends.[1]

1. For a more detailed narrative of the publishing history of *The Nursery "Alice,"* see Selwyn H. Goodacre, "The Nursery "Alice"—A Bibliographical Essay," *Jabberwocky*, Autumn 1975, vol. 4, pp. 100–19.

28 CONTRACT

Memorandum of Agreement between Charles L. Dodgson and Macmillan and Company for *A Tangled Tale*

18 November 1885
Partially printed document, with the signatures
of Dodgson and Macmillan

ONE OF SIX contracts between Dodgson and Macmillan preserved at the Rosenbach, this particular document regulates the publication of *A Tangled Tale*. The contract bears Dodgson's full signature in his characteristic purple ink, here with unusual brightness. Typical of all the existing contracts are the terms, under which Dodgson was to bear the costs of printing, paper, binding and advertising. In return he was entitled to reap most of the profits, approximately three-quarters of the selling price of the book. See section on Dodgson and A. B. Frost for further information on *A Tangled Tale*.

Alice after *Alice*

MR. DODGSON
AND MRS. HARGREAVES

> "No thought of me shall find a place
> In thy young life's hereafter—"
> —Lewis Carroll, prefatory poem
> to *Through the Looking-Glass*

EVEN AFTER the estrangement from the Liddell sisters, Dodgson completed the manuscript of "Alice's Adventures under Ground" for Alice and continued to present her with special copies of his books. On September 15, 1880, in Westminster Abbey, Alice married Reginald Hargreaves (1852–1926), whom she had met during his years as an undergraduate at Christ Church. She moved from Oxford to her husband's estate in Hampshire, where they led the life of country squire and wife, playing an active role in their community and in upper-class country society. Alice maintained close ties with her family: their visitor book is filled with visits from her siblings and their families. The Hargreaves had three sons, Alan Knyveton (1881–1915), Leopold Reginald (Rex) (1883–1916) and Caryl Liddell (1887–1955), the former two killed in the First World War. Dodgson recorded a meeting with Reginald Hargreaves in 1888, adding a rare later statement about Alice Liddell: "[I met] Mr. Hargreaves, (the husband of 'Alice'), who was a stranger to me, though we had met, years ago, as pupil and lecturer. It was not easy to link in one's mind the new face with the olden memory—the stranger with the once-so-intimately known and loved 'Alice', whom I shall always remember best as an entirely fascinating little seven-year-old maiden."[1] No documents survive recording Alice's feelings towards Dodgson in adulthood, although she published two brief memoirs in 1932 that described her childhood memories of him. Yet Mrs. Hargreaves' and Mr. Dodgson's paths did cross on occasion.[2]

1. Green, *The Diaries of Lewis Carroll*, p. 465.
2. For further information on Alice Liddell's life, see Anne Clark, *The Real Alice: Lewis Carroll's Dream Child* (London, 1981) and Colin Gordon, *Beyond the Looking Glass: Reflections of Alice and Her Family* (New York, 1982).

29 BOOK & LETTER

Lewis Carroll, *Rhyme? And Reason?*

London: Macmillan and Co., 1883
Dark blue morocco with gilt-stamped rulings and ornament

Inscribed on half-title: "Mrs. Hargreaves, with sincere regards and many pleasant memories | of bygone hours in Wonderland, | from the Author. | Dec 21/83"

Charles L. Dodgson to Mrs. Hargreaves

7 January 1892, Christ Church, Oxford

Dear Mrs. Hargreaves,
I have a favour to ask of you: so please put yourself into a complaisant frame of mind before you read any further. A friend of mine, who is in business involving ivory-carving, has had a lot of umbrella- and parasol-handles carved, representing characters in *Alice* and *Through the Looking-Glass*. I have just inspected a number of them: and, though nearly all are unsuited for use, by reason of having slender projections (hands, etc.) which would be quite sure to get chipped off, thus spoiling the artistic effect, yet I found *one* ("Tweedledum and Tweedledee") which might safely be used as a parasol-handle, without wearing out the life of the owner with constant anxiety.

So I want to be allowed to present, to the original "Alice," a parasol with this as its handle—if she will graciously accept it, and will let me know what coloured silk she prefers, and whether she would like it to have a fringe. Wishing you and yours most sincerely a very happy New Year, I am, most sincerely yours,

C. L. Dodgson

DODGSON'S EARLIEST surviving letter to Alice, dated December 21, 1883, is preserved in the collection of the Rosenbach Museum & Library. It is brief and poignant:

> Dear Mrs. Hargreaves, Perhaps the shortest day in the year is not *quite* the most appropriate time for recalling the long dreamy summer afternoons of ancient times: but anyhow if this book gives you half as much pleasure to receive as it does me to send, it will be a success indeed. Wishing you all happiness at this happy season, I am Sincerely yours, C. L. Dodgson.

THE ACCOMPANYING BOOK was this copy of *Rhyme? and Reason?*. Alice received presentation copies of many of his later books, and, as this letter some ten years later shows, the occasional *Alice*-related memorabilia.

*Mrs Hargreaves,
with sincere regards
& many pleasant memories
of bygone hours in Wonderland,
from the Author.
Dec. 21/83?*

RHYME?

AND REASON?

29. Charles L. Dodgson, inscription to Alice Hargreaves in *Rhyme? and Reason?*, 1883

Charles L. Dodgson to Mrs. Liddell

19 November 1891, Christ Church, Oxford

Dear Mrs. Liddell,

I feel that I am largely indebted to *you* (for, if the Royal party had not been staying with *you*, they would assuredly never have come near *me*!) for the unique honour I have enjoyed—enough to make me conceited for the rest of my life. There are, possibly, other commoners who have been honoured by *single* visits from Princesses: but I doubt if any others have ever had *two* visits, in one day from the same Princess!

The Latin Grammar tells us that, the more money we get, the more the love of it grows upon us: and I think it is the same with *honour*. Having had so much, I now thirst for more: and the honour I now covet is that a certain pair of young ladies should come some day and take tea with me. I have a store of ancient memories of visits from your elder daughters, but I do not think that Miss Rhoda and Miss Violet Liddell have ever even been inside my rooms: and I should like to add to my store *one* fresh memory, at least, of having had a visit from them.

If the idea is not unwelcome to *them* (which is of course essential) I think I could find enough to show them: they would be interested, I think, in my large collection of photos of little friends belonging to that very peculiar class, "stage-children."

If they felt any difficulty in coming across here, escorted only by each other, I would gladly come for them.

I do not ever ask more than *2* ladies, at a time, for tea: for that is the outside number who can see the same photographs, in comfort: and to be showing more than one at a time is simply distracting.

If I were 20 years younger, I should not, I think, be bold enough to give such invitations: but, but, I am close on 60 years old now: and all romantic sentiment has quite died out of my life: so I have become quite hardened as to having lady-visitors of *any* age!

If the reply be favourable, will they kindly choose a day, for conferring on me this coveted honour, when they have *plenty* of spare time on their hands? I do *not* enjoy brief hurried visits from my young lady friends. A couple of hours would certainly not tire *me* of *them*, however much it might tire *them* of *me!*

> Believe me
> sincerely yours,
> *C. L. Dodgson*

ALTHOUGH HIS DIARY records the occasional friendly exchange with Mrs. Liddell, Dodgson's relationship with Alice's mother had always been strained. This letter refers in the first paragraph to the visit of the Duchess of Albany, widow of Queen Victoria's youngest son Prince Leopold, and her children Princess Alice and Prince Charles Edward. Dodgson then asks for a visit from Rhoda (1859–1949) and Violet (1864–1927), the two youngest Liddell daughters, aged thirty-two and twenty-seven. As this letter indicates, Rhoda and Violet never numbered among his child-friends. When Dodgson's friendship with the elder daughters abated after 1863, the break prevented him from making overtures to the younger daughters. Neither married, so unlike their older sisters Lorina and Alice, they still lived at the Deanery in 1891. Rhoda and Violet came for tea a few days later; soon after this visit, Mrs. Liddell and Lorina did likewise. Alice came to visit her family at the Deanery a short time later, and she too received an invitation to tea. She made a brief call on Dodgson with Rhoda. It was their last meeting.

31 LETTER

Mrs. Hargreaves to Evelyn Hatch

5 September 1932, Westerham

Dear Miss Hatch

No, I have no letters left of Mr. Dodgson's and greatly I regret not having kept answers to childish letters, but I do not remember many. I am terribly sorry that I cannot help you. The collection should be an interesting one.

> Yours sincerely
> *Alice P. Hargreaves*

EVELYN HATCH edited a volume of Dodgson's letters to children in 1933. Alice's brief letter to her was in response to an appeal made to all of Dodgson's former child-friends. In her published recollections of 1932, Alice stated that Dodgson's letters were all destroyed by her mother.

BEATRICE (1866–1947), Ethel (1869–1975), and Evelyn (1871–1951), the three daughters of Oxford colleague Edwin Hatch, were among Dodgson's closest and long-lived friends. Unlike Alice, the Hatch sisters maintained their relationships with Dodgson into adulthood. As children, they were also among his primary photographic models and some of his earliest models to pose in the nude.[1]

1. Three nude photographs of the Hatches are still extant. Among the four known surviving nudes in Dodgson's œuvre—all in the collection of the Rosenbach—they are to be part of a future exhibition at the Rosenbach devoted to Dodgson's photography.

ALICE COMES TO AMERICA

"I think now my adventures overseas will be almost as interesting as my adventures underground were."
—Alice Liddell Hargreaves, 1932

IN 1928, the recently widowed Alice Hargreaves placed the manuscript of *Alice's Adventures under Ground* up for auction at the London office of Sotheby's. Many prominent book collectors were present at the sale on April 3rd, including of course Dr. Rosenbach, by now already known in some circles as the 'Napoleon of the auction rooms.' When the lot was called, The British Library engaged in spirited bidding against another private collector. Dr. Rosenbach refused to bid against the public institution, but when the Library dropped out, the Doctor purchased the manuscript for £15,400—some $75,000 at the time. Realizing the gravity of the purchase, Dr. Rosenbach immediately offered to sell the manuscript to the British Library at cost. The Library, however, could not afford the manuscript even at this price, and the now notorious Dr. Rosenbach set sail with it shortly thereafter.

DR. ROSENBACH quickly sold the manuscript to Camden collector and industrialist Eldridge Johnson, making a condition of his own: Johnson was to permit a public showing of the manuscript at the Free Library of Philadelphia. Johnson agreed and the exhibition took place to much critical acclaim, though he complained several times to the Doctor about its installation. The eccentric Johnson then retreated from the public eye, though he kept the manuscript with him at almost all times, even commissioning a special traveling case for it to be taken on his yacht. "Alice's Adventures under Ground" was to resurface only in 1932, in the presence of Alice herself, until after Johnson's death when it was given to the British Library, where it remains today.

32 NEWSREEL

Paramount News, "Alice in U.S. Land"

29 April 1932, Alice Hargreaves arriving in New York on the
    Berengaria. [Modern copy]
Courtesy of David and Maxine Schaefer Lewis Carroll
    Film Collection

ALICE HARGREAVES' adult life remained largely free of Wonderland until 1932, the centenary of Dodgson's birth. She became a patron of the charity organization Helpers of Wonderland, and gave a speech at the opening of the "Lewis Carroll Centenary Exhibition"

in London. It was in America, however, that the biggest celebration took place. Columbia University staged a major retrospective exhibition and invited Alice to journey to America to receive an honorary doctorate of literature celebrating her role as child-muse to Dodgson. Alice sailed on board the *Berengaria* with her son Caryl and her last surviving sister, Rhoda Liddell, arriving on April 29—just before her eightieth birthday. Her journey attracted considerable press attention as Americans learned there was a real Alice in Wonderland. Many of the newspapers juxtaposed photographs of Alice arriving in America with photographs by Dodgson of her as a child. These latter photographs were by then in private collections due to Alice's sale, along with the manuscript, of many of her photographs in 1928.

ALICE KEPT a journal of her trip, but her entries contain only the briefest statements of events. Caryl Hargreaves kept a livelier journal, recording the media swarm on board the ship after it arrived at quarantine in New York:

> The first thing was they wanted to photograph her, so we all climbed up to the sun deck where they took between 200 and 300 photographs of her, holding on to an immense copy of *Alice in Wonderland*, almost bigger than she is, which they had brought for the purpose. This done they proceeded to take a talkie of us. Then we went downstairs to the Palm Court again, and the reporters asked me a certain agreed number of questions which I answered, with APH [Alice Pleasance Hargreaves—Caryl Hargreaves' term for his mother in the journal] interpolating remarks occasionally.[1]

THE NEW YORK TIMES reported, "Asked for her personal recollections of the author, she replied, 'I only remember him vaguely. I recall that he was the kindest of people to small children.'"[2]

THE "TALKIE," a short newsreel to be shown as a prelude to a feature film, was unexpected, and Alice had to extemporize her answers to the reporter's questions. The headline is 'Alice in U.S. Land.' The first shot shows Alice by herself; a subsequent shot shows her seated on the deck of the ship surrounded by a group of people including Rhoda and Caryl. The dialogue is as follows:

Mrs. Hargreaves: "It is a great honor and a great pleasure to come over here and I think now my adventures overseas will be almost as interesting as my adventures underground were. I think that I have every prospect of having a most wonderful time as I had down the rabbit hole.

Man: Then it is true that you are the original Alice in Wonderland, Mrs. Hargreaves?

Mrs. Hargreaves: Well, yes, the story was told to me and my sisters. We were all in the boat together with Mr. Dodgson, who was rowing us down the river.

Man: As one who has read your book many, many times and whose children have read it, we've gotten great enjoyment from it, and I am certainly glad to meet you in person.

Mrs. Hargreaves: Thank you very much indeed.

Another man: And if I had had any children they might have read it too!

IN NEW YORK, Alice stayed in a grand suite at the Waldorf-Astoria hotel and was treated like royalty. She received her honorary degree on May 2, again described by Caryl Hargreaves:

> After an early luncheon [Columbia professor] Zanetti fetched us and took us to Columbia University for the conferring of the Honorary Degree of Doctor of Litterature [*sic*] on APH. They took her into a robing room and put a gown on her, then took off her hat and put a mortarboard on her head. Then they put the hood on for a photo to be taken of her with [Columbia president] Dr. Murray Butler. Then they formed up a procession and walked into the Library, where Zanetti introduced her with a speech, and Murray Butler made another speech at the end of which he conferred the degree upon her and they put the hood over her head. It was a very impressive scene, and APH was nearly overcome with emotion when she replied.

THE NEW YORK TIMES quoted her speech: "I thank you, Mr. President, for the signal honor bestowed upon me. I shall remember it and prize it for the rest of my days, which may not be very long. I love to think, however unworthy I am, that Mr. Dodgson–Lewis Carroll knows and rejoices with me."[3] She was then reunited with the manuscript, lent by Eldridge Johnson to the Carroll Memorial Exhibition. Two days later, on her birthday, Alice was the guest of honor at the closing ceremonies of the exhibition, where she again gave a short speech. Back at the Waldorf-Astoria, Alice was presented with a huge birthday cake with 80 candles.

1. The journal is preserved at Christ Church, Oxford. See Edward Wakeling, "Mrs. Hargreaves Comes to the U.S.A.," in Charlie Lovett, ed. *Proceedings of the Second International Lewis Carroll Conference* (The Lewis Carroll Society of North America, 1994), pp. 36–52.

2. *The New York Times*, April 30, 1932.

3. Quoted in David and Maxine Schaefer, "Alice's Adventures Overseas" *Jabberwocky*, Spring 1982, vol. 11, no. 2, p. 54.

33 PHOTOGRAPHS

W. Coulbourn Brown, Portrait of Alice Hargreaves at 2006 DeLancey Place

10 May 1932. Gelatin silver print
See illustration inside front wrapper

W. Coulbourn Brown, Portrait of Alice Hargreaves and Eldridge Johnson

10 May 1932. Gelatin silver print

ALICE and her party traveled to Philadelphia to meet with Dr. Rosenbach, Eldridge Johnson, Arthur Houghton and Morris Parrish, all great Carroll collectors. The Rosenbachs hosted a luncheon at their DeLancey Place home, only two houses from the current Rosenbach Museum. These photographs were taken in Dr. Rosenbach's library. Caryl Hargreaves noted: "We had a very good luncheon with plenty of good wine. After luncheon a great photographing of APH. E. Johnson perfectly overcome with joy because APH suggested that he should be photographed with her." Rosenbach's biographer described, "Eldridge Johnson, towering over her, had the time of his life showing off the gadget-trimmed, watertight, fireproof, portable, steel safe-deposit box which he had had made to house the precious manuscript so that it would suffer no harm as it traveled on his yacht in the tropical seas."[1]

1. John Fleming and Edwin Wolf, *Rosenbach. A Biography* (Cleveland, 1960), p. 371.

"No End of Little Girls": *Letters to Child-friends*

"So among the wonderful memories of old Oxford and its inspiring personalities our Mr. Dodgson will always hold a foremost place. And when sometimes we dream again of the quiet dignity of those streets of long ago we cannot fail to see that tall, thin, black-coated figure, his smooth-shaven face half suppressing a smile as, head erect, he strides along St. Aldate's in quest of some child-friend to whom he can give happiness."

—Beatrice Hatch, "Lewis Carroll:
A "Child-Friend's" Picture,"
The Times January 28, 1932

THROUGHOUT his adult life, Dodgson sought constantly to befriend children. He approached the children of his friends, met others on train trips and at the seaside, and sought out child-actors he admired on the stage. Dodgson nurtured his friendships—some of which lasted into the child's adulthood—through visits, games, puzzles, letters, trips to the theater or art exhibitions, and photograph sessions. Most of his child-friends were little girls, but boys occasionally attracted Dodgson's attention. As Dodgson himself got older, the little girls tended to be replaced by young women in their teens and twenties. His friendships with children necessarily involved friendship with parents, and he wrote many letters to parents asking for permission to take a child to the theater, to arrange for a photograph session, or to request a visit to Oxford or Eastbourne, where he spent many summers.

NO LETTERS written to the Liddells as children survive, but the Rosenbach preserves a number of letters cherished by other child-friends. The majority of these date to the later part of his life. Moreover, the Rosenbach collections include several letters Evelyn Hatch received and used to compile her volume of Dodgson's letters to children. The many letters in the Rosenbach collections concerning photography have not been included in the selection presented here; they are intended to be part of a subsequent exhibition focusing on Dodgson's photography.

THE LETTERS to child-friends illustrate the side of Dodgson that made him famous. Former child-friend Agnes Keith (née Hull) wrote to Evelyn Hatch that Dodgson was "the first really whimsical mind to put his thoughts on paper and the pioneer of clean, won-derful nonsense."[1] In his characteristic purple ink, used from 1870 to 1890, Dodgson negotiated for visits from his friends, gave advice, told stories, and made jokes playing on the absurdities of language and social customs. The letters show Dodgson as a kind and generous man with a unique sense of humor, but they also show a deliberate man with both clearly defined principles and an unconventional modus operandi, navigating his way through contemporary codes of propriety.

1. Letter to Evelyn Hatch from Agnes Keith (née Hull), 18 November 1933, Rosenbach Museum & Library.

34 LETTER

Charles L. Dodgson to Mrs. H.C. Raikes

6 January 1873, London

Dear Mrs. Raikes,

May I treat Alice, Amy, and Edith to a sight of "Goody Two Shoes" at the Princess' on Thursday afternoon (the 9th)? It begins at 2, & the fairy-tale part is over about 3 1/2, so that they would not be out at all later. I should not wish to keep them for the harlequinade business, as I have seen it and consider it decidedly coarse and vulgar. I should not [at] all mind undertaking them alone, but if you would prefer the governess coming too, perhaps you would treat her to *her* ticket, as it is hardly a thing *I* can offer to do.

The fairy-tale performance is quite unexceptionable and particularly well done.

Very truly yours,
CL Dodgson

I have got the three children in the house for a call, and they all send their very best love.

DODGSON HAD MET Alice Raikes and her parents in 1871 while visiting a London relative near where the Raikes lived. Three days before writing, Dodgson saw the pantomime *Goody Two Shoes* and noted in his diary that "the acting of little Katie Logan was quite extraordinary," but made no mention of the harlequinade.[1] When he took the children a few days later, they left early as promised. Pantomimes were popular theatrical entertainments generally involving magic and a traditional fairy tale. They incorporated singing, dancing, comic segments, and dramatic visual images. The harlequinade section involved the stock character of a fool. Although Dodgson adored the theater, his rigid moral standards required that he be particular about his choices. He objected vociferously to anything he thought vulgar or transgressive, and he believed strongly that any religious statements were not to be uttered lightly.

DODGSON'S REQUEST that the children accompany him alone would become typical of his later friendships with children, as several of the letters in the Rosenbach collections show. His refusal to pay for the governess stemmed from the fact that as a single gentleman, Dodgson could not respectably take a single adult woman to the theater. With the rumors about himself and the Liddells' governess some ten years before, Dodgson must have become wary of governesses as chaperones. Victorian literature testifies that governesses occupied a tricky position in society, with a status somewhere between servant and gentlewoman.

1. Green, *The Diaries of Lewis Carroll*, p. 317.

35 BOUND ALBUM OF LETTERS

Charles L. Dodgson to Agnes Hull

1877–1883
Private collection

THIS SPIRAL LETTER is one of a number written to Agnes Hull (1867–1936), the daughter of a London lawyer. The Hull family spent several summers at Eastbourne, where Dodgson met them in 1877. Dodgson found the children particularly enchanting, describing them as "delicious" in his diary, and he became friends with the entire family of parents and five children. He was soon exchanging letters with the family, staying at their London home, and taking the children to the theater. Agnes became a favorite, and Dodgson outdid himself with puzzles, jokes, and visual tricks in his letters to her over the next five years. In this letter, he refers to a manuscript book of riddles titled "Remarks on the Victims" he had put together for her. She had sent it back to him, apparently to allow him to add to it, and Dodgson teasingly complains that it had gotten damaged in the mail. Dodgson recorded in his diary in 1879, "Agnes carried off the little MS book 'Remarks on the Victims'; and probably dropped it in the road: at all events it is lost."[1] As in the last sentences of this letter, Dodgson often fussed about the strength of affection expressed in her letters and pushed Agnes to return his endearments. In 1933, Agnes Hull Keith related an anecdote that indicates a measure of youthful resistance to Dodgson's friendship: "Mr. Dodgson's rooms in Lushington Rd. [at Eastbourne] looked along to a house we had in Gildredge Rd. and he used to put a flag in his window

"when he wanted us," but I am afraid it was neglected for he waved every day and we lived among a big crowd of first cousins and friends with whom he would *not* mix and never would share us with any one."[2] The friendship ceased in 1883, when the Hulls' affection for Dodgson waned.[3]

1. Quoted in Cohen, *The Letters of Lewis Carroll*, p. 332.
2. Letter to Evelyn Hatch from Agnes Keith (née Hull), 18 November 1933, Rosenbach Museum & Library.
3. See Bakewell, *Lewis Carroll*, pp. 254–55 and Cohen, *Lewis Carroll*, pp. 227–28 for further information on the complicated circumstances of the break with the Hulls.

36 LETTER

Charles L. Dodgson to Mary and Florence Crofts

13 May 1882, Christ Church, Oxford

My dear Mary and Florence,
(Of course I feel that the above is unjustifiably arrogant, as a mode of addressing two ladies of a certain age: but then, you know, what *is* one to do when one is *told* not to "Miss" said young ladies? My nature is to do what I'm told: so I didn't Miss you while here: and it is surely needless to add that I do not Miss you now that you are gone!) There are 3 courses open to you in dealing with the enclosed piece of music. (1) The one who *is* the eldest might appropriate it. (2) The one who *looks* the eldest might do so. (3) You might fight for it. There: could Gladstone have put it better? Whichever course you take, I cannot doubt that, for many an evening to come, at 9.10 punctually, these 6 notes will be struck, with a heavy bang, 101 times in succession, in order that all your family may realise what Oxford life is like. It gives one a peaceful sort of feeling to think that one will not be there to hear it.

Yours affectionately,
C. L. Dodgson

MARY and Florence Crofts numbered among Dodgson's "rail" acquaintances. He met them on a train on July 7, 1865, noting in his diary, "Left for Oxford: down to Reading I traveled with a Mr. Crofts, wife and two little girls. Having accidentally found out that he was an old friend of Henry Kingsley's, I soon made friends with the party, and before we parted at Reading had settled that if they came to Oxford I would photograph Mary, the eldest child."[1] They did not appear in his diaries again until two days before this letter was written, when Mr. Crofts, Mary, and Florence dined with Dodgson at Christ Church. The two women were thus in their early twenties when he wrote instructing them to strike an enclosed chord on the piano 101 times. The bell 'Great Tom' was rung 101 times every evening to mark the 101 students at

morning to night, and didn't even mention, when I sign

Very well,

truly, Lewis Carroll.
Oct. 22/78.

35. Charles L. Dodgson, letter to Agnes Hull, 1878, Private Collection

Christ Church, a number constant since the 1660s. As Dodgson's rooms after 1868 were right next to Tom Tower, he had every reason to state that it would be peaceful not to have to hear it.

1. Green, *The Diaries of Lewis Carroll*, p. 232.

37 LETTER

Charles L. Dodgson to Charlotte Rix

2 September 1885, Eastbourne

My dear Lottie,

I know you are thinking all manner of bad things about me—first, because I have got your sister down here, and am taking her to various Larks (which, alliteratively, belong to *you*)—secondly, because I have not sent you a Letter (to which, alliteratively, you are entitled) for many days, if not weeks. But really I am not so bad as you think—or at any rate there are many worse. You know I often send you Love: and I was just thinking how Lucky you are to be so initialled: so that everybody must send Love. If, like me, you had 'D' for an initial, things would be Different, and I should send you 'Dislike' as soon as Look at you! Your destiny, of course, has other things in store: e.g. to be Long, and Lank, and in disposition Lugubrious. However Love outweighs all that. Now for *Edith*, I need hardly say, I can only feel Esteem: and Early walks and Education are the only articles I can supply her with: and, in both those respects she is catching it—as she will tell you when you meet. But that can't be helped: one of the deepest motives (as you are aware) in the human breast (so deep that many have failed to detect it) is Alliteration.

That's about all I have to tell you at present, except that I am Enjoying Edith a good deal—or rather, I *should* be doing so, if she were not Enjoying herself so much: but, as you know (for you are *nothing* if not Logical), it is no more possible for two persons to Enjoy the same individual than to Eat the same cherry.

> Always affectionately yours
> *C. L. Dodgson*

CHARLOTTE (1867–1952) was the younger sister of Edith Rix (1866–1918), who at nineteen sent a solution to a mathematical problem Dodgson published in the magazine *The Monthly Packet*. At the time, Edith was studying mathematics in order to attend university, and she and Dodgson began corresponding. She attended Newnham College, Cambridge, partly on Dodgson's advice, and eventually became a teacher. Dodgson dedicated *A Tangled Tale*, a collection of his mathematical problems, to her. Charlotte became an actress, probably through the help of Dodgson and Ellen Terry, to whom he introduced her.

DODGSON met Charlotte only once. Eighteen-year-old Charlotte's account of their meeting survives in a letter to her mother, making it a rare contemporary account from a child-friend rather than a memory recalled decades later.[1] She wrote of a visit from "The Great *Lewis* himself!!!" and describes their outing at length. She commented, "He has no end of little girls he has scraped up from all sorts of places, and from what he said, a lot of people that he just writes to like us. He is tall rather, thin, and no beard or moustache and his hair is rather grey; he *looks* eccentric I think and he is deaf with his right ear. He is very fatherly; calls you child."[2] Dodgson, however, wrote to Mrs. Rix about the outing, "let me confess, in confidence, that I don't think I *did* succeed, as you think, in setting Lottie 'at her ease.' I feel no doubt that, if she had *quite* felt that, she would have talked more, and not merely *replied.*"[3] This remark gives a glimpse of the kind of girl or young woman he sought for his friendships. Dodgson and Charlotte corresponded at length over several years; all of his letters to her are now preserved at the Rosenbach.

THIS alliterative letter on Charlotte ("Lottie") and her sister Edith's names was written while Edith was staying with Dodgson at his summer lodgings in Eastbourne. Edith and her mother visited Dodgson on a number of occasions at Christ Church, London, and Eastbourne. Mrs. Rix eventually allowed Edith to visit Dodgson by herself. He wrote in his diary on September 7, 1885: "Mrs. Rix left at 2:10, leaving Edith (*mirabile dictu!*) in my care till tomorrow. After the decision of Mr. and Mrs. Rix, only a week ago, that such a thing could not be thought of because of 'Mrs. Grundy,' it is rather droll to have that position entirely abandoned! It will make an excellent precedent for having other visitors, of any age up to 19."[4] "Mrs. Grundy" was a short-hand term derived from a dramatic character that personified the conservative influence social opinion had on matters of propriety. Dodgson's unorthodox friendships often led him to use this term in his correspondence and diary.

1. See Cohen, *The Letters of Lewis Carroll*, pp. 578–80.
2. Cohen, *The Letters of Lewis Carroll*, p. 580.
3. Cohen, *The Letters of Lewis Carroll*, p. 581.
4. Green, *The Diaries of Lewis Carroll*, p. 438. It is not clear why Dodgson believed the age of nineteen to be the outer limit for unchaperoned visitors, although interestingly the age of consent had just been raised from thirteen to sixteen by the Criminal Law Amendment Bill a few weeks before this diary entry. This legislative change came as a result of W.T. Stead's famous expose of child prostitution, "The Maiden Tribute of Modern Babylon," published in the *Pall Mall Gazette*. Dodgson published a letter in the *St. James Gazette* condemning Stead's sensationalistic writing, fearing the effect such lurid detail would

38. W. Kent, photographs of Edith and May Miller, 1882

have on men and boys. In 1861, the age of consent had been defined as twelve and had been raised to thirteen in the 1870s.

38 PHOTOGRAPHS

W. Kent, Portraits of Edith and May Miller

Not dated, but probably 1882. Albumen prints in blue velvet pocket-sized double frame

THIS bright blue velvet-covered pocket-sized double frame features a photograph of Edith Miller on the right and May Miller on the left. The photographs are cropped from cartes-de-visite. They were probably taken at Eastbourne in 1882, as Dodgson's diary for August 1 records that "Mrs. Miller's sister brought May and Edith to see me, and left them for me to get them photographed at Kent's."[1] Although Dodgson had given up the art himself in 1880, he often took his child-friends to professional photographers and arranged the composition. He continued to seek photographs of adult and child-friends. He treasured his collection of photographs and loved to show them to his large circle of friends.

THE WIDOWED Mrs. Miller, née Louisa Smith (1844?–1919), and her daughters Marion (or May, 1868–1946) and Edith (1870–1929) were Eastbourne acquaintances of Dodgson. His friendship with the Miller girls lasted until his death. From 1895 to 1898, Edith was a student in Oxford under the auspices of the Oxford Association for Promoting the Education of Women. She later went on to work on the English Dialect Dictionary and became a lecturer and tutor in English. Little is known about Marion's adult life.

1. Unpublished diaries of Charles L. Dodgson. I am grateful to Edward Wakeling for sharing this entry with me.

39 LETTER

Charles L. Dodgson to Edith Miller

3 September 1894, Eastbourne

My dear Edith,
   Though your crimes are such as lambs cannot forgive, nor worms forget, yet, as it happens, I'm neither a lamb nor a worm; so *perhaps* I can manage it.
   Please remember that, so long as *Beatrice* is here, it will be strictly proper for either of you to call, even alone. I think your mother will agree in this view. And, even after she has left, need you be supposed to *know* it, for a week or so?
        Your sexagenarian lover,
            C.L.D.

   P.S. I shall want to take Beatrice to the *other* theatre on Wednesday: so *you*'ll have to come too! The posters look like battles with North American Indians, and awful scenes of slaughter. You will be frightened: but never mind: you shall have 2 or 3 glasses of brandy before we start, and *then* you'll be all right.
   Please come at 5 each day, for tea. We'll have dinner about 6 1/2.

As he grew older, Dodgson increasingly characterized himself as an avuncular old man, well beyond any suspicion of romantic attachment, and pursued the company of young women in their teens and twenties more and more often. The tongue-in-cheek closing to this letter reflects Mrs. Miller's concerns about chaperonage. Edith Miller was by this date a woman of twenty-four visiting the sixty-two-year-old Dodgson. The Beatrice referred to is Beatrice Hatch, former child-friend and frequent visitor to Dodgson. Dodgson's requests of parents for visits from their daughters—sometimes women in their twenties—were, by his own admission, unusual. Still, if he felt his actions conformed to his own rigid standards, he did not let the opinions of others deter him. Consequently, he played what reads as a finely tuned performance with his young women-friends and their parents in order to negotiate the desired visits. Dodgson professed no interest in marriage and deflected any questioning by noting that at his age even young women seemed like children to him. Several child-friends later recalled that he had indeed treated them like children when they were well into adulthood.

The somewhat flippant tone of this letter suggests Dodgson's specific frustration with Mrs. Miller. A number of letters in the Rosenbach collection to Edith Miller contain jabs at her mother's stringent rules. A few days earlier, he recorded in his diary, "Dear May Miller was engaged to dine with me: but Mrs. Miller wrote to say there was so much 'ill natured gossip' afloat, she would rather I did not invite either girl without the other. No doubt it is Mrs. Richards' doing: she means well, but it is a pity that she should interfere with other people thus." Although it turned out that Mrs. Richards had not gossiped about Dodgson, Mrs. Miller still objected to visits with one sister alone. A few days later, he recorded that he "wrote to Edith Miller that I will expect May on Tuesday, and her on Wednesday, to dine while Beatrice Hatch is here. (It is the only way I can now have them to dine! As Mrs. Miller now won't let them come singly, and *I* won't have them together.)"[1] Edith too must have expressed concern over visiting and Dodgson replied with this letter, the opening sentence of which refers to Dickens' *Martin Chuzzlewit*. The visits took place as Dodgson wished.

1. Cohen, *The Letters of Lewis Carroll*, p. 1034, n. 1.

40 LETTER

Charles L. Dodgson to Dorothy Joy Poole

11 November 1896, Christ Church, Oxford

What shall I call thee?
"I happy am—
Joy is my name."
Sweet Joy befall thee!"

There, my dear Dorothy; if you happen *not* to have seen these lines before, and if you can guess, *from the style*, who wrote them, I will admit that you are a fairly good judge of modern poetry!

Having now allowed a year or two (more or less) to elapse, in order to give you time to recover your courage, I write to ask whether you are disengaged for next Saturday evening, and, if so, whether I may fetch you, at 6 1/2, to one of my grand dinner-parties.

Do not be alarmed at the *number* of guests: it will be .99999, etc. It *looks* alarming, I grant: but circulating decimals lose *much* of their grandeur when reduced to vulgar fractions!

Two things need to be mentioned.

One is, evening-dress is *not* expected. I wear morning-dress *myself:* so why should my guests be more ceremonious? (I do so *hate* ceremony!)

Another is, what do you usually drink at dinner? My lady-guests *mostly* prefer draught-lemonade. But you can have any of the following beverages:

(1) bottled lemonade;
(2) ginger-beer;
(3) beer;
(4) water;
(5) milk;
(6) vinegar;
(7) ink.

Nobody has yet chosen either No. 6 or No. 7.

By the way, "morning dress" includes morning-*shoes* (or boots). So don't bother yourself to bring *evening*-shoes, unless it is a positive discomfort to you to wear the others. In that case, perhaps the *best* thing to bring would be a pair of those lovely morocco *slippers,* with fur-edges. (N.B. I once tried to buy such a pair, for myself: but only got the crushing reply that "slippers of *that* kind are *only* worn by *ladies*"!)

Affectionately yours,
C. L. Dodgson

41 LETTER

Charles L. Dodgson to Mrs. Poole

16 November 1896, Christ Church, Oxford

Dear Mrs. Poole,

I fancy I did thank you, in anticipation, for the loan of Dorothy for an evening: but I now wish, in retrospect, to send a *double* measure of thanks, for the treat you have given me, and for the hope that I have se-

thing, to bring would be a
pair of those lovely morocco
slippers, with fur-edges.
(N.B. I once tried to buy
such a pair, for myself:
but only got the crushing
reply that "slippers of that
kind are only worn by
ladies"!)
            Affectionately yours,
                C. L. Dodgson.

Ch. Ch. Nov. 11/96.

What shall I call thee?
  "I happy am —
  Joy is my name".
Sweet Joy befall thee!

    There, my dear Dorothy;
if you happen not to have
seen these lines before, and
if you can guess, from the
style, who wrote them, I
will admit that you are
a fairly good judge of
modern poetry!
    Having now allowed a
year or two (more or less) to
elapse, in order to give you
time to recover your courage,
I write to ask whether
you are disengaged for
next Saturday evening, &,
if so, whether I may fetch

40. Charles L. Dodgson, letter to Dorothy Joy Poole, 1896

cured a new *real* child-friend. She has good *sense*: she is a pleasant and interesting companion: and I like her. (I do not fear that this last avowal will suggest any such question as "What are your *intentions?*") Now I wonder whether *you*, encouraged by the circumstance that your daughter has returned alive, will brave the ogre's den, and come and dine with me? Child-society is very delightful to me: but I confess that grown-up society is much more interesting! In fact, *most* of my "child"-friends (specially those who come to stay with me at Eastbourne) are now about 25.

I wonder if you and Mrs. Aubrey-Moore will ever allude to your acceptance of an invitation which *she* declined? If so, it would be an amusing discussion to overhear! I rather *think* she will be simply *horrified* at the laxity of your views about the chaperonage of young ladies! I enclose a book for Dorothy, with my love, and am sincerely yours

C. L. Dodgson

My only engagements are Tu. and Th.

IN JUNE AND JULY of 1896, Dodgson lectured on symbolic logic at the Oxford High School for Girls. Dorothy "Joy" Poole (1882–1947), born into an academic family, was one of the few young women who attended. After finishing the lectures, Dodgson attempted to continue a friendship with three of the girls, Dorothy Poole and Margery and Kate Aubrey-Moore. As with Edith and May Miller, Dodgson had to confront the problem of chaperonage. He was unsuccessful in gaining the consent of Mrs. Aubrey-Moore to dine with her daughters singly. Dodgson's letter to Mrs. Poole, however, met with her approval, and so he dispatched this humorous invitation to thirteen-year-old Dorothy. Mrs. Poole herself dined with Dodgson two weeks later.

Games, Stories, Puzzles, and Other Books

"He would teach us to do puzzles, and he would talk with us (not *to* us)."

—Kate Terry Gielgud,
Kate Terry Gielgud: An Autobiography

ALONG WITH VISITS, photography and the theater, an important aspect of Dodgson's relations with children lay in storytelling, games and puzzles. Dodgson developed a repertory of logic puzzles and illustrated stories that he used to entertain children, but his letters are remarkable for their breadth of invention of puns, teasing, and witticisms. For a man who wrote hundreds and hundreds of letters to children over the course of decades, he seldom repeated himself. He was always ready with fresh acrostic poems, riddles, and puzzles. He devised several games such as a complicated version of croquet and a board game. He also invented a number of word games, such as Doublets and Syzygies, that appeared both in magazines and in book form, which he then distributed to his young friends.

42 BOOK & LETTER

Lewis Carroll, *Doublets*

London: Macmillan and Co., 1880. 2nd edition
Red cloth with gilt lettering on board and spine
Inscribed on half-title: "To A.J. Lewis
   with the Author's sincere regards."

Charles L. Dodgson to Charlotte Rix

18 April 1885, Christ Church, Oxford

My dear Lottie,

   (. . . .) The enclosed game is very popular with some of my young friends: it is much better when played by *2 sets* than by *2 players*: the players in each set consult in whispers, so that it is a very conversational game.

   Yours affectionately,
   C. L. Dodgson

   To change one word of a Doublet into another, you must change one letter at a time, by putting a new letter into its place, and always making a real word.

   e.g. | HEAD | heal | teal | tell | tall | TAIL

   The intermediate words are "Links," and, the fewer links you use, the more glory you get. The above has 4 links, however you do it: at least *I* can't do it with less.

   "DOUBLETS" became Dodgson's most popular word-game, one he humorously described as a "form of verbal torture." As Dodgson demonstrates in this letter to Charlotte Rix, the game is simple: take a word and transform it into another by creating a chain of real words that changes one letter at a time. Macmillan published this small 'Alice red' cloth-bound book version for Dodgson. The book describes the rules of the game and provides lists of doublets for the reader to solve. To aid the reader, a sizable glossary of words comprises the second half of the book. As with his other books, he soon presented his friends with their own copies. The Rosenbach copy was given to A.J. Lewis, husband of Kate Terry and father of Kate Terry Gielgud (née Lewis). This second edition is a larger format version of the first edition published the year before.

43 CASE & PAMPHLET

Lewis Carroll, *Wonderland Postage-stamp Case and Eight or Nine Wise Words About Letter-Writing*

Oxford, 1890. Inscribed: "May Miller, from the Inventor. 20/5/90"
See illustration overleaf

ONE of Dodgson's own forays into the mass-marketing of Alice items was this 1889 stamp case, which provided a convenient way to sort stamps of different value. The front cover shows Alice holding the Duchess's baby. Upon pulling the case out, the baby turns into a pig. The back cover likewise shows the grinning Cheshire cat; the inside shows the cat beginning to fade from view. The case additionally included a tiny pamphlet, *Eight or Nine Wise Words About Letter-Writing*, with humorous advice on how to write efficiently, neatly and politely. The essay also explains the letter-register Dodgson began using in 1863. Because Dodgson wrote several letters a day, he kept track of letters sent and received by designating each with a number and providing space to summarize a letter's contents. Now lost, the letter-register at Dodgson's death had 98,721 entries for letters sent and received. Dodgson consulted his letter-register often in his correspondence. For example, in a letter to Charlotte Rix, he referred to his letter-register to clear up a mistake he made in thinking that Mrs. Rix had suggested he introduce Charlotte to Ellen Terry. He found that he had offered to introduce Charlotte to Ellen Terry two years before in an entry he quotes as "March 22, 1887. *Mrs. Rix*, offering, if she approves, to take Lottie to call on Ellen Terry."[1]

1. Letter from Charles L. Dodgson to Charlotte Rix, 10 April 1889, Rosenbach Museum & Library.

To change one word of a Doublet into another, you must change one letter at a time, by putting a new letter into its place, & always making a real word.

e. g.

```
H E A D
h e a l
t e a l
t e l l
t a l l
T A I L
```

The intermediate words are "Links"; &, the fewer links you use, the more glory you get. The above has 4 links, however you ~~do it~~ : at least I can't do it with less.

42. Charles L. Dodgson, letter to Charlotte Rix, 1885

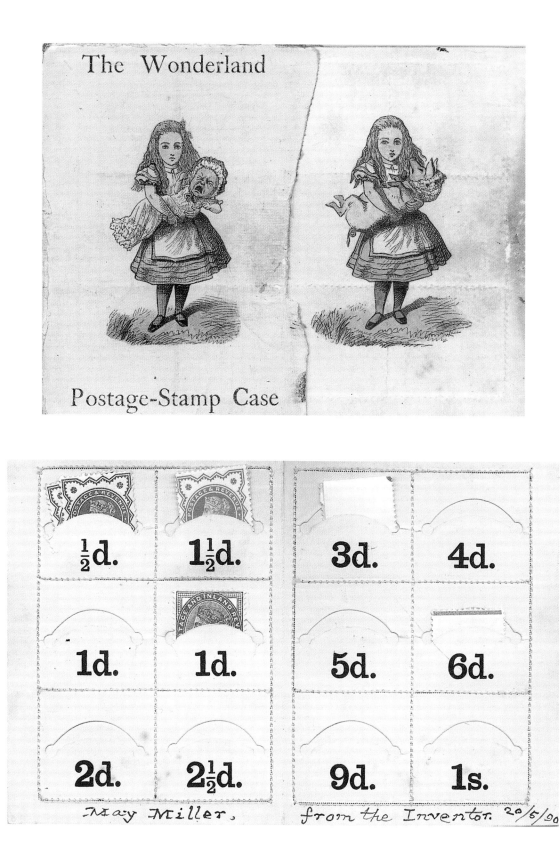

43. Lewis Carroll, Wonderland Postage-stamp Case, with interior showing stamps, 1890

44 BOOK

Lewis Carroll, *The game of logic*

London and New York: Macmillan and Co., 1887
Red cloth with gilt lettering on front board and spine
Inscribed on half-title: "Evelyn Hatch, | from the Author. | May
14, | 1894."

MUCH MORE complicated than *Doublets*, *The Game of Logic* attempted to make formal deductive logic accessible through funny examples. Dodgson hoped the mixture of logic and stories would provide an entertaining way of learning. The book came with its own set of counters and a diagram with which to play. This first edition was presented to Evelyn Hatch. Published by Macmillan and Company, the book had a publishing history similar to *Alice's Adventures in Wonderland*. Dodgson suppressed an unsatisfactorily printed first edition and sold it to an unsuspecting America.

45 TYPESCRIPT & MANUSCRIPT

Charles L. Dodgson, *Memoria Technica*

1888. Cyclostyle with a hand-lettered title

Charles L. Dodgson, Manuscript fragment with examples of Memoria Technica

Not dated

DODGSON had a lifelong interest in the ancient art of memory. This short typescript (the cyclostyle being essentially an early incarnation of a typewriter) has little to do with the architecturally-based models for memory developed by Quintilian and Cicero, however. Dodgson's *Memoria technica* replaces digits with letters as a means of memorizing dates and other numbers. The system relied solely on consonants, so that vowels could be added as necessary to create words (or even rhyming couplets) that related to the digits to be replaced. Each numeral could be replaced by two of the twenty consonants in the alphabet. The number four, for example, was represented by both 'f' for 'four' and 'q' for 'quatuor.'

IN THE RELATED manuscript fragment, the couplet

"Columbus sailed the world around,
Until America was FOUND"

yields '492'—short for 1492—alongside other examples of the technique.

46 MANUSCRIPT

Charles L. Dodgson, "When a.y. and I.a told . a . . ie . . ."

Not dated
See illustration overleaf

AN EXAMPLE of the kind of puzzle tailor-made for his child-friends, Dodgson sent this verse puzzle to the three Watson sisters, Georgina (Ina, b.1862), Mary (1861?–1928), and Harriet (Hartie), child-friends Dodgson met at Guildford. As in his acrostic poems, Dodgson plays on the children's names, here omitting the consonants in all proper names and nouns. The missing words are Mary, Ina, Hartie, creature, wings, Hartie, fairy, Ina, Mary, Mary, Ina, Hartie, party, arithmetic.

47 LETTER

D.C. Earle to Evelyn Hatch

22 March 1933, Salford
With manuscript of her recollection of a story told by Dodgson

Dear Evelyn

Bee [Beatrice Hatch] tells me you would like the story I remember Mr. Dodgson telling me as I sat on his knee and he drew the picture with a fountain pen on the back of an envelope. I treasured the drawing for many years. Alas! the story is not much written down—his voice and stammer, his delicate acting of every detail, the gradual increasing of the picture—but I remember the climax was grand for I had no inkling of what the drawing would represent when turned but a firm belief in the reality of the robbers.
    Yours very sincerely
    D.C. Earle

DOROTHY CHARLOTTE EARLE (1874–1942) was the youngest daughter of John Earle, Professor of Anglo-Saxon at Oxford. Dodgson became acquainted with the children of the family in the early 1880s and the friendship continued through the 1890s. Earle's vivid memory of the story decades later, written in response to Evelyn Hatch's appeal, attests to Dodgson's skill at storytelling to children.

48 BOOK

Lewis Carroll, *The Hunting of the Snark: an Agony, in Eight Fits*

London: Macmillan and Co., 1876
Red cloth with gilt-stamped picture cover
Inscribed on half-title: "Kate Terry Lewis | from the Author | Mar. 29. 1876"

IN ADDITION to the two *Alice*s, Dodgson published many other books with Macmillan and Company. As Charles Dodgson, he produced mathematical works including his last, unfinished project, *Symbolic Logic*. As Lewis Carroll he produced collections of comic and serious poems and two more fictional works for children.

When .a.y and I.a told .a..ie they'd seen a
   Small ..ea.u.e with .i..., dressed in crimson and blue,
.a..ie cried "'Twas a .ai.y! " Why, I.a and .a.y,
   I should have been happy if I had been you!"

Said .a.y "You wouldn't." Said I.a "You shouldn't ——
   Since you can't be us, and we couldn't be you.
You are one, my dear .a..ie, but we are a .a..y,
   And a.i...e.i. tells us that one isn't two."

46. Charles L. Dodgson, manuscript puzzle for the Watson sisters, not dated

Next to the two *Alice*s, *The Hunting of the Snark* is his best-known work. The lengthy nonsense poem was first illustrated by Henry Holiday, whose drawing decorated both sides of the book's binding, as in this presentation copy given to Kate Terry Gielgud (née Lewis, the daughter of Kate Terry and A.J. Lewis, niece of Ellen Terry, and future mother of Sir John Gielgud). The ordinary binding was gray cloth with the Holiday illustrations stamped in black. The red and gold binding of this copy was one of several special bindings Dodgson had made. Like *Alice*, this poem was associated with a child-friend, Gertrude Chataway, whose name forms the basis of the dedicatory acrostic poem.

49 BOOKS

Lewis Carroll, *Sylvie and Bruno*

London and New York: Macmillan and Co., 1889
Red cloth with gilt-stamped picture cover
Inscribed on half-title: "Mrs. R.G. Faussett | from the Author |
    Feb. 22. 1890"

Lewis Carroll, *Sylvie and Bruno Concluded*

London and New York: Macmillan and Co., 1893
Red cloth with gilt-stamped picture cover
Inscribed on half-title: "Evelyn Hatch, | from the Author. |
    Jan. 30, | 1894"

THE TWO PARTS of *Sylvie and Bruno* were Dodgson's only other major works written for children. Not a critical success when first published in 1889 and 1893, their popularity never did rival the two *Alice*s. Yet Dodgson was extremely proud of the two books in which he attempted to impart a more serious message to children than can be found in the *Alice*s. Beginning in 1867 with a short story, "Bruno's Revenge," Dodgson slowly expanded the work over the years, even inventing some of it during storytelling sessions to various child-friends. He then commissioned Harry Furniss to illustrate it; the books were bound in 'Alice red' cloth with gold picture medallions after Furniss's drawings. The dedicatee for *Sylvie and Bruno* was Isa Bowman, a child-actress who became one of Dodgson's closest child-friends in his later years. The dedicatee for *Sylvie and Bruno Concluded,* was another close child-friend, Enid Stevens. Dodgson presented this first edition of *Sylvie and Bruno* to Mrs. R.G. Faussett, the wife of a fellow mathematician at Christ Church. He presented this copy of *Sylvie and Bruno Concluded* to Evelyn Hatch.

A Tangled Tale: *Dodgson and A.B. Frost*

". . . you are *the* man, of all the artists I know of (now that Tenniel is past hoping for) whose help I should wish to have."

—Letter from Charles L. Dodgson
to A.B. Frost, 25 April 1881,
Christ Church, Oxford

"Now let me say how *intensely* I admire what you have done. The drawing is perfect, & exquisite to a degree which one *very* rarely finds in woodcuts."

—Letter from Charles L. Dodgson
to A.B. Frost, 30 January 1879,
Christ Church, Oxford

WITH JOHN TENNIEL no longer available to illustrate his works, Dodgson was forced to seek other illustrators. He found a young and conscientious artist in A.B. Frost, a native Philadelphian. Frost claimed to be largely self-taught, but he studied briefly with Thomas Eakins at the Pennsylvania Academy of the Fine Arts. Frost's work came to Dodgson's attention in 1877, when the artist traveled to London. Dodgson commissioned Frost to illustrate his 1883 *Rhyme? and Reason?*, a book of comic poems, and his 1885 *A Tangled Tale*, a book of narrative mathematical problems. Frost went on to become a popular illustrator in America, with drawings appearing in several magazines. His most famous works remain his original illustrations of Uncle Remus, Brer Rabbit, and other animal characters for Joel Chandler Harris's books.

THE Rosenbach Museum & Library preserves a number of Frost's sketches and finished drawings for the illustrations to *Rhyme? and Reason?* and all 39 extant letters from Dodgson to Frost. A selection is given here. The letters chronicle their entire professional relationship. Dodgson recorded their first meeting in his diary for 1878: "Paid a long visit to Mr. Frost, whom I had not seen before. He showed me two blocks done for the 'The Three Voices,' which are deliciously funny and extremely well drawn."[1] Their correspondence continued amicably for several years, during which time Dodgson gave up photography and his post as Mathematical Lecturer and devoted his energies to work on literary projects such as *Sylvie and Bruno* and *Symbolic Logic*. Frost produced a total of 65 finished drawings for *Rhyme? and Reason?* over the five intervening years, initially in England and later in Philadelphia. Dodgson was not an easy task-master. He had his own ideas for the illustrations to his poems, and he sometimes sent sketches he expected

Frost to follow. Their relationship ended when Dodgson harshly criticized Frost's work for *A Tangled Tale*.

IN ADDITION to discussion of Frost's drawings, Dodgson's letters address varied topics such as finance and photography. Dodgson occasionally offered the American detailed advice on English customs. On April 12, 1878, he wrote Frost

I notice that you have not guessed (and no wonder) that my address is 'Rev. C.L. Dodgson.' If you won't mind my mentioning it, the English form of address, where one is not 'Rev.,' is, 'So-and-so, Esq.' *not* 'Mr. So-and-so.' The usage is really a curious anomaly: my friend leaves his card on me as 'Mr. J. Smith,' and I begin my letter to him 'Dear Mr. Smith,' but I *direct* it 'J. Smith, Esq.' I should only write 'Mr. J. Smith' if he were a tradesman. I am almost afraid of mentioning these trifles, for fear you should think I had taken offence at being directed to as 'Mr.' Nothing could be further from my thoughts.

DODGSON'S THOUGHTS on the physical beauty of the child's form are another point of discussion. Dodgson manifested his interest in children not just in his friendships with them, but in his admiration for images of children, both clothed and nude. In this, Dodgson was not unique among Victorians, although his interest was extreme. The Victorians developed a veritable visual mania for children. Not only did artists cover the walls of art exhibitions with paintings of children, but they invented the market for the image of the child through the nineteenth-century proliferation of children's books, magazines, advertisements, and greeting cards. One of Dodgson's frankest statements about representations of children occurred in a May 7, 1878 letter to Frost: in asking him to draw a child, he requested

a shaded pencil drawing, a study from life, (but *not* a Cupid,) that I may keep it as a specimen of your power in drawing a beautiful figure. As it is *not* for publication, you need not put an atom of drapery on it, and I can quite trust you, even if you made it a full-front view, to have a simple classical figure. I had rather not have an adult figure (which always looks to me rather in need of drapery): a girl of about 12 is *my* ideal of beauty of form. A pretty *face* would be a pleasant addition, but by no means essential: a beautiful *form* is what I should specially like to have as a specimen of your skill.

JUST AS DODGSON had to navigate through the waters of Victorian propriety when it came to chaperones, he likewise dealt with the difference between public morality and taste and his own private standards, standards which he would have described only in aesthetic rather than sexual terms.[2]

1. Green, *The Diaries of Lewis Carroll*, p. 371.

2. Questions concerning the character of Dodgson's sexuality certainly arise from his statements such as this one. See Dodgson's biographers for further consideration of Dodgson's inner life and sexuality.

50 LETTER

Charles L. Dodgson to A. B. Frost

7 January 1878, Christ Church, Oxford

Dear Sir,

(. . . .) Let me introduce myself as the writer of a little book (*Alice's Adventures in Wonderland*) which was illustrated by Tenniel, who (I am sorry to say) will not now undertake woodcuts, in order to explain my enquiry whether you would be willing to draw for me a few pictures for one or two short poems (comic) and on what sort of terms . . .

DODGSON APPROACHED Frost for the first time in this letter after noticing his illustrations in a magazine. Throughout their ensuing correspondence and cooperative efforts, Tenniel was held up to Frost as an ideal model. Dodgson solicited Tenniel's opinion of Frost's work and even repeated Tenniel's words to him in a letter of February 7, 1878:

The designs of Mr. A. B. Frost appear to me to possess a certain amount of quaint and grotesque humour together with an *uncertain* amount of dexterous drawing, which might no doubt be developed into something very much better, but which is at present—as it seems to me, judging by the book—somewhat crude and commonplace in execution; but the pictures are obviously very slight, and perhaps it is hardly fair to give an opinion.

51 DRAWING, MANUSCRIPT & BOOK

Charles L. Dodgson, Sketch for "A Game of Fives"

Enclosed in letter to A.B. Frost, 20 April 1883
Pen and ink on paper
See illustration overleaf

Charles L. Dodgson, "A Game of Fives"

Not dated. Manuscript poem sent to A.B. Frost

Lewis Carroll, *Rhyme? and Reason?*

London: Macmillan and Co., 1883
Green cloth with gilt-stamped picture cover
Inscribed on half-title: "CLD [monogram] | received Dec. 6/83."

THIS IS ONE of several sketches Dodgson sent Frost as a model for illustration. Frost did not however adopt Dodgson's idea and instead produced three separate illustrations for the poem. Dodgson omitted one of these and even altered another, the small illustration of the young girls. He wrote to Frost on July 31, 1883:

you will be glad to know that, after all, I have used the head-piece for 'A Game of Fives': in my last I told you the children were not pretty enough. My chief objections were to the mouths of the two full-faces, which were heavy and shapeless, and sadly turned down at the corner, and to the right eye (*her* right—the left in the picture) of the one partly hidden by the baby, which was too far from the other, and too high up in the forehead. But, on second thoughts, I ventured on doctoring the drawing a little: I erased the turned-down corners, and made the upper lip of the kneeling child more shapely: and as to the wandering *eye*, I ventured to cover it up altogether and draw it again lower down. I hope you will forgive my having taken such liberties with your drawing.

52 LETTER

Charles L. Dodgson to A. B. Frost

16 June 1884, Christ Church, Oxford
Contemporary copy made by Dodgson

Dear Mr. Frost,

Your welcome letter reached me on the 9th of June. Before I answer it, let me remind you of my request, made July 31, 1883, that you would make out a new account for the pictures—for which purpose I sent all the necessary details. I want to know exactly how we stand, tho; there is no need for you to *pay* any thing: it can go to my credit in our next account.

I am very glad indeed to know that you will be able to begin work for me after Aug. 1: before which date I hope to send you one or two of the incidental poems, which can be illustrated quite independently of the story, and as grotesquely as you like. The story itself I will get to work at as soon as I can: there is a lot of material ready, but it needs arranging: and it may easily happen that I may not be able to keep you fully and continuously supplied; so that I am very glad to know you have other commissions you can at any time take up.

51. Charles L. Dodgson, sketch for "A Game of Fives," pen and ink drawing, 1883

As to the "children" difficulty: I only want *two* for this book, a girl of 12 and a boy of 6. They ought to be pretty, certainly, and *not* so ancient-looking as (for instance) the crying children atop p. 59. Could you choose a suitable nephew and niece, and send me a little study of each, and I would tell you if they suited my ideas. If all fails, there is still the possibility of leaving blanks for the children, and I would get Miss E. G. Thomson (who draws lovely children) to put them in. While on the subject, I hope you won't mind my criticising the lady-likeness of the young lady at p. 183. She looks a little too much like a barmaid. Should any lady occur in the story, I should desire a little more refinement. Du Maurier's ladies, in Punch, will give an idea of my meaning, tho' of course I don't want you to imitate any other artist.

I sent off a presentation copy of "Rhyme? and Reason?" for you, by book-post, on June 11th. I hope it may reach you safely, but I fear there are many risks of robbery on the way, and there have been many complaints lately of things disappearing when sent by post to other parts of the world. The book on "Folklore," which you said you would send, has not yet appeared.

It will give me great pleasure to make the acquaintance of Mrs. Frost when you bring her over the water.

Believe me,
Very sincerely yours,
C. L. Dodgson

DODGSON had been very pleased with Frost's work for *Rhyme? and Reason?*, suggesting on April 25, 1881 that he try his hand at serious pictures for a companion volume of *Rhyme? and Reason?* that would contain Dodgson's serious poems. But this did not appear until 1898 as the posthumous *Three Sunsets*, with illustrations by Emily Gertrude Thomson. Dodgson had previously stated his intention to Frost to write another children's book:

I have a grand scheme in my head, that I want you to hold yourself engaged for—as you are *the* man, of all the artists I know of (now that Tenniel is past hoping for) whose help I should wish to have. It is to write another child's book—I have a good deal of material for it already, and I think I can manage *one* more without repeating myself and making people say "It is only a repetition of Alice". The pictures would require the same *sort* of skill that Tenniel showed in "Alice", and would include beautiful children and comic monsters. I feel sure you would illustrate it superbly, and I think it would be more worthy of your skill than this volume of poems, of which I have a very low opinion.

I think fairy-tale is more in my line of work than poetry.

THIS PROJECT eventually became the two volumes of *Sylvie and Bruno*, illustrated in the end by Harry Furniss. Frost did begin working on the project in 1883, but this letter implies that after the problem with "A Game of Fives," Dodgson was no longer convinced of Frost's ability to draw pretty children. He wrote on October 26, 1883: "I lament the difficulty you complain of in getting child-models, and that you cannot draw them without. For I should *much* like you to illustrate a fairy-tale for me: but a pretty child would be *essential*. Won't advertising and liberal pay produce a model?"

53 LETTER

Charles L. Dodgson to A. B. Frost

24 February 1885, Christ Church, Oxford
Contemporary copy made by Dodgson

BEFORE SENDING Frost poems so he could begin the illustration of what would become *Sylvie and Bruno*, Dodgson decided to reprint a series of mathematical problems in story form he had published in the magazine *The Monthly Packet*. He asked Frost to undertake ten illustrations for the book, each to illustrate a problem, or "knot." Dodgson sent his usual detailed instructions of what he envisioned for the illustrations. Frost began work on these drawings in August and sent the finished drawings to Dodgson in December 1885. After so much praise of Frost's earlier work for him, however, Dodgson was unhappy and wrote a lengthy letter to Frost with harsh criticisms (partially quoted below). He consequently abandoned the idea of having Frost illustrate *Sylvie and Bruno* and later commissioned Harry Furniss instead.

Dear Mr. Frost,

My long delay, in writing about your drawings for "A Tangled Tale," has been partly due to want of time, but chiefly to want of courage to enter on the subject: I fear it is inevitable that much of what I have to say *must* be displeasing to you. Let me beg pardon beforehand for this, and plead the necessity of saying what I have to say, *somehow*, though perhaps I may fail of saying it so inoffensively as it might be said by others.

I had better make the general remark to begin with, and get it over, that I fear I cannot use *any* of them in their present state. In neatness, and finish, and clearness of drawing, these seem to me to fall as far short of the average of what you drew on paper for the former book, as those in their turn fell short of what you drew on wood. To make my meaning clear, I had better begin by asking you to put before you either "Alice" or the "Looking Glass," and to examine the details of any one of the pictures with a magnifying-glass: and then to do the same thing with one of the best that you drew for me on wood, (say the one at p. 42). You will then understand what I mean (whether you agree with it or not) when I say that yours is a little, but not very far, behind Tenniel in delicate finish. He seems to me to use much fewer lines than you, but to produce a neater result.

[. . . .]

I hope you will some day forgive me this unwelcome letter.

> Yours very sincerely,
> *C. L. Dodgson*

P.S. I think I would rather *not* criticise "Stuff and Nonsense" [a book of Frost's humorous sketches published in 1884]. The fun turns too exclusively on depicting brutal violence, terror, and physical pain, and even death, none of which are funny to me.

P.P.S. I enclose a leaf of a child's picture-book, which, though a mere rough sketch, yet gives a very fair idea what a graceful English girl *does* look like.

We must, I fear, abandon the idea of illustrating a Fairy-Tale [*Sylvie and Bruno*].

FROST EVIDENTLY took offense at Dodgson's scathing criticisms. Dodgson's last extant letter to Frost, July 1, 1885 begins

> Dear Sir: (I feel I cannot, in common courtesy, persist in a form of address which *you* have discarded) I deeply regret (as I said, by anticipation, in my last) that any remarks of mine should displease you: but I think no good would be done by discussing your letter in detail, or by mooting the question whether the change has been (as you think) in my views of your style of drawing, or (as I think) in the drawing itself."

DODGSON CONCLUDED by settling their account. Frost and Dodgson apparently had no more contact after this exchange, but *A Tangled Tale* appeared in 1885 with six drawings by Frost. The book was not well received by the critics.[1]

1. See Cohen and Gandolfo, *Lewis Carroll and the House of Macmillan* for more details, in Dodgson's letters to Macmillan, of the publishing history of *A Tangled Tale*.

54 DRAWING

A. B. Frost, Sketch of a ghost and a chair for Lewis Carroll, *Rhyme? and Reason?*

Not dated, but circa 1879. Pen and ink on paper

THIS PRELIMINARY pen and ink sketch of a ghost hiding behind a chair was made for Canto I of Dodgson's poem "Phantasmagoria." In a letter to Frost on January 30, 1879, Dodgson asked for a selection of ghosts from which to choose:

> As to the "little ghost", I find it very hard to make suggestions: I should like to see a few rough sketches to select from. My idea of him is of a little old man, dressed in long frock-coat, long flowered-waistcoat, silk stockings, buckles—in fact a sort of Charles I style: with an anxious frightened look (except in the latter part of the poem, when he has recovered his confidence, where he should wear an impudent grin). But I think your sketches will be the best guide. I hope you will succeed in inventing some startling varieties of ghost for all the different species I have named!

IN FROST'S SKETCH, the ghost nevertheless has a boyish appearance. The final drawing shows an older ghost with a segmented, almost insect-like body.

55 DRAWINGS

A. B. Frost, "O hush thee gentle popinjay," unpublished drawing for Lewis Carroll, *Rhyme? and Reason?*

Not dated, but 1878-83. Pen and ink on paper

A. B. Frost, Preliminary sketch of the popinjay

Not dated, but 1878-83. Pen and ink on paper

THESE ARE TWO of several studies Frost made for a scene in Dodgson's poem "The Lang Coortin." The poem concerns a ridiculous old man who tries to court a younger woman. Frost's drawing is an unused variation on the scene in which the man drops to his knees to beseech the woman's favor, but is interrupted by her squawking bird and barking dog. In the final illustration, the man has become older and more comical and the dog—restrained by a leash made from rings sent by the suitor—lunges more sharply.

FROST'S INTEREST lay primarily in the popinjay, whose figure is transformed in the various drawings. In the larger drawings, the bird has spiky, disheveled feathers. A marginal sketch or 'remark' on the same sheet shows an almost pelican-like creature. An earlier sketch in broad strokes was a very quick attempt, probably one of many, to take a different approach to the popinjay.

55. A.B. Frost, "O hush thee gentle popinjay," pen and ink drawing, 1878–83

Charles L. Dodgson, Sketch of ghost with pillow

Enclosed in letter to A.B. Frost, 5 April 1881
Pen and ink on paper

Lewis Carroll, *Rhyme? and Reason?*

London: Macmillan and Co., 1883
Green cloth with gilt-stamped picture cover

DODGSON INCLUDED this sketch in his April 5, 1881 letter responding to Frost's drawing of a man threatening a ghost with a warming-pan for the poem "Phantasmagoria." He wrote

> The enclosed picture is the solitary exception to the collection you have sent: and I candidly admit I do *not* like the man in it. I will try to put my reasons into an intelligible form. He is, to my mind too *real* in his anger to be funny. If you were illustrating "Oliver Twist", such a man would be quite in character for "Bill Sykes murdering Nancy". And the warming-pan (taken in connection with his savage expression) is too really murderous a weapon. The little ghost begging for mercy is perfectly charming—but the man has 'murder' written in his face, and would terrify young readers more than amuse them. Also I don't think his night-shirt (though of course quite proper) is at all an artistic costume. I think he ought to be a gentle man who has been terrified and worried into unusual violence, which should be preposterous and burlesque: also I think a pillow or bolster would be more hopelessly useless for exterminating ghosts, and therefore more comic than a warming-pan, which would really be a very deadly weapon. I can't draw, myself (a remark which the enclosed sketch makes quite superfluous), but this will perhaps give you a better idea, than words alone would, of what I have in my head. I hope you will be able to patch the drawing with a bit of paper, so as to save the trouble of drawing a new ghost.

FROST DULY CHANGED the warming-pan into a pillow as Dodgson suggested.

Further Reading

Michael Bakewell, *Lewis Carroll: A Biography* (London: William Heinemann Ltd, 1996).

Anne Clark, *Lewis Carroll: A Biography* (New York: J. M. Dent, 1979).

Anne Clark, *The Real Alice: Lewis Carroll's Dream Child* (New York: Stein and Day, 1981).

Morton N. Cohen, ed. with the assistance of Roger Lancelyn Green, *The Letters of Lewis Carroll*, 2 vols. (London and New York: Oxford University Press, 1979).

Morton N. Cohen and Anita Gandolfo, *Lewis Carroll and the House of Macmillan* (Cambridge: Cambridge University Press, 1987).

Morton N. Cohen, *Lewis Carroll: Interviews and Recollections* (London: Macmillan, 1989).

Morton N. Cohen, *Lewis Carroll: A Biography* (New York, 1995).

Morton N. Cohen, *Reflections in a Looking-Glass: A Centenniel Celebration of Lewis Carroll, Photographer* (New York: Aperture, 1998).

Stuart Dodgson Collingwood, *The Life and Letters of Lewis Carroll* (New York: Century Co., 1898).

Stuart Dodgson Collingwood, ed. *The Lewis Carroll Picture Book* (London, 1899).

Rodney Engen, *Sir John Tenniel: Alice's White Knight* (Aldershot, England: Scolar Press, 1991).

Martin Gardner, *The Annotated Alice* (New York: C.N. Potter, 1960).

Helmut Gernsheim, *Lewis Carroll, Photographer* (London: Max Parrish & Co., Ltd., 1949). Revised edition (New York: Dover Publications, 1969).

Colin Gordon, *Beyond the Looking-Glass: Reflections of Alice and Her Family* (New York: Hodder and Stoughton, 1982).

Roger Lancelyn Green, ed. *The Diaries of Lewis Carroll* (New York and London: Oxford University Press, 1953).

Michael Hancher, *The Tenniel Illustrations to the Alice Books* (Columbus: Ohio State University Press, 1985).

Evelyn Hatch, *A Selection from the Letters of Lewis Carroll to his Child Friends* (London: Macmillan, 1933).

Anne Higonnet, *Pictures of Innocence: the History and Crisis of Ideal Childhood* (New York and London: Thames and Hudson, 1997).

Derek Hudson, *Lewis Carroll: An Illustrated Biography* (London, rev. ed. 1976).

James R. Kincaid, *Child-loving: The Erotic Child and Victorian Culture* (New York and London: Routledge, 1992).

Lewis Carroll (London: The British Council, 1998).

Lewis Carroll, an exhibition from the Jon A. Lindseth Collection of C.L. Dodgson and Lewis Carroll (New York: Grolier Club, 1998).

Carol Mavor, *Pleasures Taken: Performances of Sexuality and Loss in Victorian Photographs* (Durham and London: Duke University Press, 1995).

Justin Schiller and Selwyn H. Goodacre, *Alice's Adventures in Wonderland: An 1865 Printing re-described* (Privately printed, 1990).

Stephanie Lovett Stoffel, *Lewis Carroll in Wonderland: The Life and Times of Alice and Her Creator* (New York: Harry N. Abrams, 1997).

Edward Wakeling, ed., *Lewis Carroll's Diaries, the Private Journals of Charles Lutwidge Dodgson*, 4 vols. (Luton: Lewis Carroll Society, 1993-98).

Sidney Herbert Williams and Falconer Madan, *The Lewis Carroll Handbook*, rev. by Roger Lancelyn Green (1962) and Denis Crutch (Folkestone, Eng: Dawson, ca. 1979).

DESIGN   Greer Allen
TYPESETTING   John J. Moran
COLOR PRINTING   Thames Printing Company
BLACK PRINTING   Mark One Printing Co.
BINDING   Mueller Trade Bindery